PRAISE FOR
TEACHING KIDS TO BE KIND

"Very relevant in rai today. Rachel points out that your acticed daily. This book is a necess children and this book teaches yo

, creator of *The Hutch Oven*

"We live in a fast-paced world where children are often pushed extremely hard, and told that all that matters are tangible outcomes like grades. Kindness has been traded in for competition. I appreciate how *Teaching Kids to be Kind* circles back to what's truly important in life. How we communicate, how we make others feel, and how we care for ourselves should be at the forefront of what we teach our kids. This is truly a guidebook for raising wonderful human beings."

—Ali Katz, author of *Hot Mess to Mindful Mom*

"Rachel does a tremendous job of sharing the essence of kindness and what it truly takes to raise our children to be kind. As a mother, aunt, teacher and mentor, I love how Rachel mentions that kindness begins with us, the caregivers. This book is full of incredible, sound advice. The book is beautifully and simply laid out, making it both easy to read and understand. I highly recommend this book to any future parent, current parent, caregiver, teacher or mentor who want to help raise a generation of world changers . . . all starting with kindness!"

—Hope Comerford, author of *Mom Hacks* and editor of the *New York Times* bestselling Fix-It and Forget-It series

TEACHING KIDS
to Be *Kind*

TEACHING KIDS

to Be Kind

A Guide to Raising Compassionate and Caring Children

RACHEL TOMLINSON

FOREWORD BY DR. JUSTIN COULSON

Skyhorse Publishing

This book is dedicated to my daughter, Marni.
In a world where you can be anything, be kind.

CONTENTS

FOREWORD

◇◇

W hen I was a young boy—probably around eight years of age—my father taught me a lesson that still affects me today. Dad was a "milko." Back in the 1980s, his job was to deliver milk from door to door. He drove a little milk van. And I'd regularly travel with him, helping drop the milk at each home along the route.

One evening as we headed home along a quiet gravel back road, Dad slowed the van and peered quizzically over the steering wheel into the dark ahead of us. Gradually, we ground to a halt, stopping just short of a lump or mound of something in the middle of the road. The lump was a man.

Cautiously, Dad opened the van door and stepped onto the road. "Stay in the car, Justin," he warned. And then, "Hey mate, are you okay?" There was no response.

Dad took tentative steps toward the man, eventually arriving by his side and finding him half-conscious and fully drunk. Dad's best guess was that the man had been on a bender at the pub down the road. It seemed that the man had thought better of driving and tried to walk home, but he'd gone the wrong way and collapsed, wasted, in the middle of the road and was sleeping it off on the gravel.

With great effort, Dad lifted the man to his feet and carried him to our van. He opened the rear sliding door and heaved him into the refrigerated rear of the van. Dad checked the man's wallet, found his license and address, and then climbed into the front of the van with me. We drove to the man's home, where Dad carried him to the front door, rang the doorbell, and handed him over to an embarrassed, anxious, and grateful wife.

It's possible that my dad's kindness saved a life that night. But it did more. I not only learned what to do when someone needs help. I also learned what *not* to do.

Dad could have used the man's unsafe, unhealthy, unwise choices to teach me about the dangers of alcohol. But instead of pointing a judgmental finger and using the man's poor choices as an example of what not to do, my dad taught me a moral lesson of a completely different kind. My dad showed me an example of how to treat others who need help, even when their difficulty is of their own making.

While researching for this foreword, I came across a quote from a church leader, Jeffrey R. Holland, who said:

When a battered, weary swimmer tries valiantly to get back to shore, after having fought strong winds and rough waves which he should never have challenged in the first place, those of us who might have had better judgment, or perhaps just better luck, ought not to row out to his side, beat him with our oars, and shove his head back underwater. That's not what boats were made for. But some of us do that to each other.

It's easy to say, "Well that's what you get for being silly." It's easy to moralize, take the holier-than-thou position, and ignore the struggles of others. But that's not kind. And it doesn't help or teach our children anything.

However, when we witness kindness, it elevates our souls. It builds us and inspires us to be better, especially when it is undeserved. Joseph Wirthlin said, "Kindness is the essence of greatness and the fundamental characteristic of the noblest men and women that I have known." I believe him. What a powerful precept to pass on to our children.

We live in a world where it is easy to become discouraged. There is so much unkindness. Our politics, our sports, our news, driving on our roads, social media: everywhere we turn, there are examples of terrible unkindness, malice, and enmity. But while unkindness makes the news, we should not be fooled. Kindness is *everywhere*. And kindness can be in our homes, our hearts, and our children's hearts as we practice the principles in this book.

In *Teaching Kids to Be Kind*, Rachel Tomlinson has thoughtfully crafted a kindness masterclass for parents and families. Her ideas are sound. They're practical. And they have the power to help you in your quest to curate the noble character strength of kindness in your kids.

I commend Rachel and her book to you. It's a beautiful book. And it will help us create an even more beautiful world.

The philosopher Jean-Jacques Rousseau, asked, "What wisdom can you find greater than kindness?"

My answer—and the answer you'll find in Rachel's book—is that kindness is a profoundly wonderful answer. It's an answer we need. It's an answer that will set our children on the path to a lifetime of happiness and personal fulfillment.

—**Dr. Justin Coulson**
Member of the Australian Psychological Society (MAPS)

INTRODUCTION

B ecoming a parent is one of the toughest, yet most rewarding things you will ever do, and the relationship you have with your child is one that demands huge amounts of patience, dedication, compromise, and love. After you have your baby, one of the scariest moments is when you realize you won't be handed an instruction manual as you leave the hospital. When I clicked my baby into her car seat and drove out of the parking lot of the birthing center, I looked at my husband and said, "Why did they just let us leave with her? We could be anyone!" Then the crushing enormity of what we were about to undertake hit me: it was entirely up to us to care for and shape this tiny, hungry, pooping bundle of joy into a person.

Parenting is an unending series of moments made up of victories and failures, heartfelt memories and challenges, trials and errors. You have to learn how to navigate the uncharted waters of parenthood without a map, while also figuring out who you want to become as a parent. How do you want to raise your child? What values do you want to instill in them? What expectations and hopes do you have for their future? There is no parenting handbook for this, as the answers are unique to every person and family, yet it is one of the most challenging aspects of being a parent.

As a psychologist, I have specialized in working with children and families, and despite having worked with hundreds of clients throughout the years, there is one key similarity in all families across the board. Nearly every parent who has come into my office has spoken to me about the pressure they feel to raise children who are happy and who will become "good" people. Traditional parenting resources tend to focus on key child developmental stages like their physical and cognitive abilities. These books and websites give you a benchmark of whether your child is achieving things at the "right" stage and time and give you a clear idea of what is coming next. Understanding these milestones is important, but the hidden pressures of parenting and child-rearing aren't covered so well. Two key pressures—raising happy and good children—can pull parents in opposite (and very confusing) directions, as sometimes, what makes children happy doesn't necessarily translate into them being particularly good or compassionate people. In my work over the years, I have found that the key in balancing these two things comes down to developing and encouraging kindness in children.

WHY IS BEING A GOOD PERSON SO IMPORTANT?

One particular parenting pressure is about helping your child become a good person. But why is this so important to parents? Let's consider what "good" means to you. It can (and does) differ between people but generally refers to those who are **intrinsically**

good and those who demonstrate **kindness**. These are attributes that help our children to do well and succeed, because being kind helps children develop social awareness and empathize with others. Being able to understand and consider the feelings of others alongside the ability to cooperate is associated with improved relationships, general life satisfaction, and lasting well-being. In particular, children who learn to be compassionate and empathetic benefit developmentally, show more **pro-social** behaviors, and have higher self-esteem and an improved outlook on life.

> **Key Definitions**
>
> **Pro-social**—doing what is socially acceptable and appropriate
> **Intrinsically good**—good for the sake of being good. Not just to be self-serving or to be rewarded.
> **Kindness**—generally describes a person's actions or behaviors that are compassionate, generous, empathetic, and genuine.

HOW DO WE NURTURE AND DEVELOP LONG-LASTING HABITS OF KINDNESS IN OUR CHILDREN?

So, what does kindness mean to you? The definition is likely to differ somewhat between people, but in essence, it is being a moral, generous person who is genuinely concerned for others. But don't confuse being kind with being nice. Nice is about how other people see you, whereas kindness is about how you see yourself, including whether you are being true to the values you hold. Kindness is about finding compassion and **empathy** for another person while also respecting your own needs and boundaries.

Kindness is not something that is taught; it's learned from observation and experience. The challenge is that you cannot teach kindness in the way you teach arithmetic, spelling, or reading, as there is no blueprint or set of instructions for how to teach someone to become kind. Kindness is intangible, complex, and involves more than just being able to say "Please" and "Thank you" or holding open doors for people. It is easy to think that our children will naturally be kind if we are "nice to them," but in reality, it is more complicated than that. Simply put, children don't become happy by *receiving* kindness; they become happy, well-adjusted, enriched people by being *givers* of kindness.

> **Key Definitions**
> **Empathy**—being able to understand another person's emotional perspective or how they might feel about a situation/scenario.

The good news is that children are born with an innate sense of compassion and are hard-wired to be **altruistic**. The reason that altruism is innate is because human beings are socially driven, and cooperation or looking after the well-being of others is key to thriving within a group. Being altruistic is deeply rooted in human nature and is essential to the survival of the species, because it helps us work together for a common goal and look out for one another. Studies have even shown that being kind results in our brains being activated in the reward and pleasure sections. This creates a drive to want to be kind or altruistic again to feel the same sense of reward, so the pattern repeats and reinforces the importance of caring and looking after others.

However, there are competing instincts, and people are also hard-wired to be selfish to ensure their own survival. So, the challenge of teaching our children to be kind also needs to focus on how to evoke

> **Key Definitions**
> **Altruistic**—the desire for other people to be happy and being able to put another person or group's welfare before your own.

altruism over being selfish. This is a trial, because children are **egocentric**, and, at times, other developmental forces can counteract or supersede this drive to be kind and empathetic, so their primary drive is to have their own needs met first. This is totally normal, by the way. . . . Trust me, I'm a psychologist.

> **Key Definition**
>
> **Egocentric**—prioritizing and caring only for your own needs over the needs of another person or group.

WHAT ARE OTHER CHALLENGES TO YOUR CHILD'S NATURAL, ALTRUISTIC QUALITIES?

Modern society can directly challenge the ability for our children to grow up and become kind adults. These difficulties are predominantly a by-product of our technology-dependant, individually focused, consumer-driven society. We live in a culture obsessed with the idea of being an "individual," a culture focused on individual worth and self-attainment, often at the cost of the collective (Me versus Us culture). In addition to this, technology is swiftly improving, and this has naturally increased the range and accessibility of information. While this can be incredibly positive, it may also expose our children to disturbing, violent, and mature content beyond their capacity to process; this includes the potential ramifications of cyber-bullying. Technology also feeds into our "on-demand culture" due to the availability of smart technology and the Internet. Any question, need, or want is so easily attainable. When children don't learn how to wait, they don't develop the ability to delay gratification, and this can negatively impact on their ability to regulate their emotions and develop self-control. And while it may be accepted or even tolerated that children might behave in this way if they do not learn these skills in childhood, they become adults who continue to behave in the same way. This self-serving attitude can make it incredibly difficult for them to demonstrate kindness toward others because they are solely focused on themselves and their own needs.

Teaching your child to be a kind person is one of the most important jobs you have as a parent. Many parents are overly focused on their child's academic success but can forget to put their time and effort into nurturing the emotional and social well-being of their child. Today's society is very much "Me, me, me!" and encourages selfishness and instant gratification, so nurturing your child to be a good person is important in balancing the negative impacts of our materialistic world. Kindness is the antidote to this egocentric world we live in, and it encourages people to be considerate, friendly, and generous. Kindness shows a certain warmth, compassion, and respect for others. Although there are many other things that parents want for their children, kindness is actually at the core of a lot of other positive traits or ambitions we have for our kids. Research shows time and time again that repeated acts of kindness improve self-esteem, create better and more fulfilling relationships, increase a person's ability to deal with adversity, and also result in improved immunity and physical well-being. I have worked with hundreds of families and parents over the years . . . and I can say, without a doubt, that parents ultimately want their children to find happiness—and kindness is the answer.

WHO MIGHT USE THIS BOOK AND HOW IT CAN HELP YOUR CHILD LEARN TO BE KIND

It is really important for me to acknowledge who might use and find this book beneficial. Although I refer to "parents" throughout the book, this term is referring to all caregivers who take any responsibility for the well-being of a child. For me, this means formal and informal caregiving arrangements, as well as kinship and other shared caregiving roles, right through to teachers, mentors, and other influential people in a child's life. Regardless of your title, or DNA that links you to a child, you are here, reading this book, because raising a kind child is important to you.

The ability to be kind is influenced by many things, including a person's temperament, genetics, and their lived experience. In particular, the parent-child relationship is key in a person's early experiences and it shapes their personality, self-esteem, and social and emotional intelligence . . . all of which are important factors in being able to demonstrate kindness. This is where you come in! Your role as a parent is essential, and supporting your child to be a compassionate person will allow them to navigate their social world with ease and will maximize their happiness, which is something that most parents strive for. This book explores some of the challenges to raising kind children, especially in a world full of turmoil, violence, and instant gratification. However, it also focuses on many of the different, practical and specific ways that you can encourage kindness and altruism in your child. The majority of the tips have been amended or adjusted to fit the different developmental stages of children. The tips can be followed "to the letter" or they can simply serve as inspiration for you and your family. You can follow them in order, or pick and choose based on the daily life and needs of your family. Regardless of how you choose to use this book and tips, the aim is to incorporate kindness into your child's world every day, so that kindness and compassion become the norm and the expectation.

You might benefit from keeping a journal while working through the activities in this book. Record your thoughts, feelings, and reactions to the discussions and tips I have included. Your reflections will help deepen your understanding of what kindness means to you, the values you want your child to develop, and your own experiences of being intentionally kind in your daily life. If writing isn't your thing, that's okay! You can draw, paint, or start a conversation with a friend or family member. It doesn't matter how you go about it; the point is to get into the nitty-gritty detail of your ideals as a parent.

This book is also suitable for toddlers right up to adolescents. Many of the tips give an alternative for older or younger children, or their developmental level. I have shared stories and tips suited for a variety of ages and abilities simply because it is never too late or too early to introduce intentional kindness into your family and to children.

There are five key strategies that I will explore in this book, which clearly outline how you as a parent can help your children learn to be kind. After exploring each of these key guidelines to raising caring and respectful children, another chapter follows with clear tips that outline how you can put these strategies into practice within your family. It might be tempting to skip ahead directly to the tips, but I encourage you to read the outlines first to give some context and understand of why these activities are going to help your child learn to be kind.

- **Modeling:** This is known as "walking the walk" and explores the important role you play in demonstrating what kindness looks and feels like to children.
- **Talking the Talk:** Learning to be kind is influenced by the way you speak to your child(ren), the power of the language you use to describe or talk about them (and others), and how important it is to develop positive self-talk in children.
- **Managing Destructive Feelings:** An element of developing kindness is also centered around a child's ability to regulate their own emotions (when faced with a challenge) and also delaying their own gratification to meet the needs of others (including individuals as well as groups).
- **Rewards:** This does not refer to rewarding your child for everyday demonstrations of helpfulness, but rather how to encourage and support kindness.
- **Expanding Your Child's Circle of Concern:** This explores the impact of taking children (within reason) outside their comfort zone and exposing them to different cultures and ways of life. It is an important element in building empathy, tolerance, and kindness, expanding their concern from themselves right out into wider systems including family and the wider community.

Each of these broader strategies will be accompanied by specific tips that outline how you can put these ideas into action in really practical ways to help you develop kindness, compassion, and empathy in your child. I have used my experience with families to shape and guide the activities and information included in this book. The tips are inspired by conversations and sessions with real families who have used these ideas to not only build their child's potential, but also their relationships with one another. I have developed 365 tips for you to implement. This is because genuine compassion is not about one single act, or self-serving behaviors, it is about demonstrating kindness every day of the year.

CHAPTER 1
MODELING

WALK THE WALK

Ever had one of those days? You know, the kind of day where everything seems to go wrong, or just seems to grate on your very last nerve? You pour your morning coffee and realize the milk is sour, you want a hot shower and the water is freezing, you are now running late for work, and your child spends twenty minutes looking for their school shoes (one of which is found in the freezer and the other is located hanging from a tree in the back garden), and when you finally leave the house and slam the front door behind you, you realize you have locked the car keys in the house. Cue facepalm and possibly some choice swear words.

Sometimes life can be tough, and it's normal to struggle with challenges or stressful events that life can throw at us. Even with the best intentions, we might get tired and snap, or react negatively, in ways that don't necessarily fit with what we expect (or hope) from ourselves. Our children watch us as we respond to frustrations, and over time this forms a template or example for how to react or manage when they are struggling. As a parent, you are probably already aware of this fact, and it can be incredibly confronting to see your child mimicking some of the not-so-pleasant things they have seen from either you or others in their immediate family or friendship circle. The thing is, as parents, we aren't perfect and that's okay! But sometimes we don't react in ways that are really in line with what we expect from our children in regards to values, morals, or ideals. Parents often explore with me that they feel guilty because they haven't been particularly kind, patient, or forgiving at times when they are stressed themselves—in short, they aren't able to demonstrate the kindness that they are trying to instill in their children. When this happens, I think it is important to recognize it within ourselves. Instead of focusing on fault or difficulties we are facing, we should acknowledge the strength it takes to address these challenges and face them head-on. As adults, we also know that life isn't always going to go our way, so rather than reacting in the heat of the moment, we need to take charge and practice reacting in a way that is more in line with our own values or morals (and, in turn, what we expect from our children).

Throughout their life, your child is reliant on you to show them what is expected of them. Some of this is through the rules and boundaries you put in place, but mostly, your child will learn by how you treat them, others, and yourself. So, no pressure, parents! I am simultaneously joking and entirely serious at the same time. Modeling is an integral way that we instill morals and values in our children; this includes their understanding of, and desire to be, kind to others. Early exposure, practice, and modeling of kindness is incredibly important in building your child's desire to be good without any other agenda. It starts with your child observing your actions and using them as a template for how they should interact with the world around them. Their first demonstration of altruism provides them with positive feelings that increase their desire to keep being kind. With reinforcement and encouragement, they will begin to be able to anticipate and meet the needs of others, and soon it will become intrinsically rewarding to be kind (wanting to be kind for the simple fact of being kind and not for any other reason).

WHAT DOES KINDNESS FEEL LIKE?

One of the key elements in teaching our children kindness is showing them empathy and compassion so they learn what kindness feels like. Empathy is being able to understand someone else's emotional experience, or, to put it simply, being able to step into someone else's shoes. This is a key skill associated with being kind, and it takes courage and strength. If people are empathetic, they can understand another's perspective, which allows them to act appropriately to support them. When you are able to show your child that you truly understand their perspective and can hold them in that space, it is a powerful experience. Imagine that one day your child comes home from school in a flood of tears because they had a fight with their best friend. Instead of rushing to fix the issue with practical ideas, you express that you can see how sad they are and perhaps even ask if they would like to talk or have a cuddle. This lets your child know that you have noticed how they feel and that their feelings are important. Also, by just holding them (in an emotional sense) in this space, you are letting them know that their feelings are perfectly acceptable and normal, and you aren't accidentally minimizing their feelings by rushing to find practical solutions.

Empathy is a skill that can be developed. Your child will benefit from being exposed to and witnessing your empathy toward them and others. It can also be strengthened by filling your child's "bank of knowledge" about human experiences so that they can use this information and apply it. Essentially, you want them to be able to understand other's perspectives and also what emotions feel like so they can interpret social situations and respond compassionately. This involves a lot of discussions, narrating your own experience, and asking questions to raise their awareness of a wide range of emotions and get them noticing other people.

> **Key Definition**
>
> **Hold (holding)**—in a therapeutic setting, holding someone's space is all about accepting and understanding someone's experience without judgment or shame. It is about creating a sense of unconditional regard/acceptance.

To teach empathy, we need to have some understanding of how people connect or tune in to others' emotional experiences. Having this knowledge can help shape the kinds of questions you might pose to your child or pinpoint important discussions. One example is seeing somebody else cry because they are being picked on or teased. Simply seeing someone else being sad can be enough to make you feel sad, too. You connect the emotion: I'm feeling sad, so that must be what they are feeling, too. The other way we connect empathically is when we use our knowledge or perspective to consider what we have learned in the past. We then use this knowledge to compare it with what is happening in front of us. Using the same example above, you see someone cry because they are being teased, you visually identify that they are crying and notice that it is because they are being teased. So, you make the mental connection that they might be sad because they are being teased.

But why all this fuss about empathy? Being empathetic is not only kind, but it also makes people happier within themselves. As a parent, this is essentially what you want for your child: you want them to be happy, and empathy is incredibly important in this regard. Empathetic people have stronger personal relationships that are meaningful and supportive; this is thought to be because of what they offer other people and what they expect in return—compassion, kindness, respect, and understanding.

WHAT DOES KINDNESS LOOK LIKE?

Besides showing your child what kindness feels like, they also need you to model what it looks like. It's easy to ask our children to be kind or to display compassion, but if they don't see us demonstrate it, it's hard for them to follow the rules we set. In my work throughout the years, I have spoken to dozens of parents who were in despair about their child's behavior: shouting, outbursts, and/or swearing (among other things). I can recall one mom who brought her little boy for counseling who reported feeling mortified about some challenging behaviors he was displaying, in particular swearing. She told me lots of wonderful things she had been trying in order to support more appropriate behavior in her child but she had yet to see any progress and was worried about why his challenging behaviors were persisting. After a number of sessions, I overheard her in the waiting room speaking to someone on the phone, and she was swearing, though not in a crude way, more for emphasis. Please know that this was not a terrible mom; she had just forgotten her son was listening. However, her behavior was not consistent with what she was asking from her son, and this was one major reason that, as a family, they were having difficulty stopping him from swearing.

This highlights that simple encouragement of our children isn't effective if they don't see us leading by example. This is true for most behaviors, including kindness. Children need to witness kindness and experience it themselves so that they learn how worthwhile it is to be kind to others. It's easy to believe that simply *being* kind to our child is enough; however, we may forget to apply this ideal to others in our lives (family, friends, strangers), and all this does is confuse our children. It can be relatively easy to be kind to your child, for example; you might understand that their age or developmental stage will require patience from you in regard to the way you interact with them or what you expect from them. However, this same level of patience might not be extended to everyone in your world. Your partner or significant others in your life might cop your frustration when you come home from a long day, or you might be in a rush or running late and perhaps you growl at your older children to move them along quicker. It is very normal to have different expectations for various people in your life, but this can be a little confusing for children who tend to have black-and-white, or concrete thoughts about things.

It might also be easier for you to be kind to people who you know and care about as opposed to strangers. Although there might be many valid reasons behind your actions, if your child witnesses these inconsistencies, they may learn that not everyone should receive, or be deserving of, their kindness. It is for that reason that this chapter and subsequent tips are so important and why the message of kindness needs to start with you.

BOUNDARIES AND RULES

Some confuse being kind with being passive, but this isn't true. In fact, at times, being passive can be incredibly damaging as it can mean that your boundaries, values, and needs are being ignored or disregarded to meet the needs of someone else. We don't want to instill this in our children: that being kind means they are a doormat. So, an important element of teaching children to be kind is also showing them how to maintain firm and appropriate boundaries as well as respecting the boundaries of others. If children are shown by their parent(s) how to consistently and lovingly put boundaries in place, they experience a number of positive outcomes, including increased self-sufficiency, confidence, social satisfaction (more friends or mutually beneficial relationships), and happiness.

Throughout my years as a psychologist, I have met many parents who feel that by putting in boundaries, they are upsetting their children or impacting their happiness; but this is misguided . . . lovingly misguided. Children need their caregivers to give them rules and be consistent with them: it helps them feel safe and confident as their world is predictable—they know what to expect and they feel contained. It also sets very clear expectations or rules around behaviors and attitudes that they display. If you want to set them up to become kind, then your boundaries should be in line with this expectation. If something is unacceptable once, then it should always be unacceptable, or your child should have a very clear idea about how to apply the rules and boundaries you are setting. Even if your child is tired, had a tough day, or it's their birthday, the rules still exist! Children who feel safe are better adjusted emotionally and socially, so how can you model and enforce appropriate rules for your child?

Family Rules

Rules and boundaries help create structure and give a clear indication about what behaviors you expect from your child. These rules can be general (respect, honesty, etc.) or specific (put your dirty clothes in the hamper, don't swear, etc.), but the key is consistency, regardless of the origin of the rule. As you start to read the tips that this book offers, you will see how rules and boundaries are put into practice and everyday life. *But why are rules so important?*

Essentially, rules are the building blocks that teach children what is "okay" versus "not okay," and these early family rules will help teach your child that there are other places and circumstances where they need to follow instructions or guidelines. Being able to follow rules and social expectations will help them demonstrate kindness toward others as they learn how to curb their own impulses and gratification for the needs of the group or to help someone else. It is perfectly normal if your child tests these rules; as a parent to a toddler, let me tell you that regardless of my professional knowledge and skill, my daughter still tests the boundaries. And it's also completely normal that some days I want to tear my hair out. Although this can be frustrating for you, when your child does test the boundaries, the response they get helps them learn about their world, their role in it, and what others expect of them. Also, just be aware that if they are young, they might simply forget a rule or set of instructions. So, the key here is your consistency, ongoing teaching, and how you respond to them testing or bending the rules. Without consistency, children become confused about what is expected of them (which may lead to acting out, challenging emotions, lack of confidence, etc.) and they can also come to realize that if they behave in a certain way, there are no repercussions—neither of which are helpful if you want your child to learn to be kind.

Consistency is challenging, especially if you are tired, distracted, or busy. Sometimes in the moment, it can be easier to just give in and let it slide. If you are a two-parent household or have a shared parenting arrangement, then maintaining consistency can get even more complicated because everybody needs to be on the same page. *So how can all of your family members get on the same page?* The next chapter will explore some specific tips you can follow as a family; however, below is an overview of the key steps regarding rules that are helpful to understand first.

- First, every family is different—your needs, values, and goals are different—so your family rules will be equally diverse. Once you figure out what you stand for as a family, it's easier to figure out which rules are the most important to you.
- Don't have too many rules! People make the mistake that a whole bunch of rules will make for better-behaved kids, but this isn't really the case. If you are too rigid, it doesn't allow children to learn from their mistakes, or they may rebel against these very strict guidelines. Try to focus your family rules on the "non-negotiables"—the things that your family just cannot function without.
- Communication is key! Make sure that everyone who plays any role in caring for your child, including extended family,

friends, etc., know your stance and are willing to back you up and be consistent with the rules you have put in place.

- Remind your children of the rules. Younger children in particular may just forget the rules, and we need to give them a break because they are learning so many new things. It can take multiple, consistent responses for them to really "get" it and take the new information on board.
- Rules need to be age- and developmentally appropriate. If you ask too much from your child or put a rule in place that they cannot follow yet (for developmental reasons, like expecting a newborn to say please and thank you) all this does is dent their confidence and instill a low sense of self-worth.
- If you set rules that are consistent and age-appropriate, your child is going to feel a heightened sense of achievement and confidence because they know they can meet your expectations, which gives them a sense of pride.

FORGIVENESS

When you make a mistake, it's important to admit that you were wrong and seek forgiveness. We cannot expect ourselves to be perfect all the time, or that we will never be at fault, because of course we are human, and we should never expect this of our children either. When you can be strong enough to admit you were wrong, and demonstrate what an appropriate response could have been, you are showing your child that it is okay to be wrong and it does not make them any "less"—it is not shameful, nor does it cost them anything to apologize. If you are at fault, modeling contrition after making a mistake can teach your child how to respond positively in the future and give them opportunity to see mistakes as learning opportunities.

You can also model the "giving" of forgiveness. This in itself is a type of kindness: being able to genuinely forgive and show compassion when someone has made a mistake. When your child or someone else in your life responds negatively or inappropriately to a frustration or life challenge, don't come down on them too hard. Forgiving is not easy, but without your compassion, they may struggle with feelings of guilt and shame. You can also use this opportunity to teach your child some alternate, positive responses and recover from the unpleasant feelings of having made a mistake. It is imperative that children know what forgiveness feels like so that they understand why it is so important to give it.

DON'T FORGET! BE KIND TO YOURSELF

Your child also notices how you treat yourself. Are you overly critical of your failures or mistakes? Do you consistently put yourself last or miss out on things because you are putting everyone else's needs before your own? Unfortunately, many parents have incredibly high expectations of themselves, which in and of itself isn't a bad thing, as our expectations make us strive to improve and "do better." However, these expectations are often unrealistic, and all this does is make good parents feel guilty that they aren't perfect. It's impossible to be perfect all the time. Trust me on this!

Parents feel a huge amount of pressure to put others first to show that they care about them. However, you can use up all your energy doing this, so it is easy to become reactive, irritated, and then snap. As a result, you feel guilty or embarrassed and are more likely to try and recommit even more emotional and physical energy toward caring for your loved one(s). This depletes you even further, and it makes it even harder for you to summon up the mental reserves, patience, and energy to parent consciously and positively, so you snap because you feel over-burdened, tired, worn out . . . and so the cycle continues.

I really want to get a megaphone and shout from the rooftops that **"Self-care isn't selfish!"** because so many parents struggle with this concept and feel like they will be judged for looking after their own health and well-being. It's as though they feel that self-care somehow takes away from their ability to look after their loved ones. I have to tell you that sentiment is entirely false and stops people from seeking help or looking after themselves properly. Self-care is actually an essential element of daily life, as it allows you to be a more kind, present, and patient parent, which is something most parents want.

> **Key Definition**
>
> Self-care: an intentional way that we look after our emotional, mental, and physical health.

So, what is self-care exactly? I like to explain it to my clients by giving the following analogy; for anyone who has flown on an airplane, try and recall the safety demonstration. The flight attendants tell you that if the oxygen masks are deployed, you need to fit your own mask first before you help anyone else. This really goes against many people's first instinct to protect their loved ones. However, the reason you are asked to fit your own mask first is because if you don't have enough oxygen, then you can become confused and unwell, and will not able to adequately protect your family (or yourself!). This is the same premise as self-care: if you don't look after yourself first, it is nearly impossible to adequately care for your loved ones.

Parenting can be a tough gig, so don't forget how important it is to be kind to yourself. If we don't cut ourselves enough slack, or if we berate or judge ourselves for making mistakes, how on earth can we expect our children to accept their own (very normal and human) mistakes. Kindness is not just about being compassionate toward others, but it's also integral for well-being and confidence to be kind to ourselves. From a very early age, we all develop an internal dialogue about ourselves and what we are worth. We want to help our children develop a voice that is gentle and self-accepting, so we need to model for them how we treat ourselves kindly, as well as others.

REFLECTION EXERCISES—WALKING THE WALK

1. Be honest with yourself and explore what your go-to response is when frustrated. Do you go silent? Rant and rave? Become snippy or irritated? Bottle it up?

2. Now spend some time thinking about how you would prefer to react to frustration.

3. What kinds of expectations do you have for your child when they are expressing their frustration?

4. How do you treat yourself when you have made a mistake? Are you compassionate or critical?

5. Think about the expectations you have for yourself. Are they realistic or similar in any way to what you expect from others?

6. Do you practice any kind of self-care?

7. Where do you place yourself in the hierarchy of the family in terms of importance?

CHAPTER 2
TIPS FOR MODELING

1. Write down a few things you love and value about your child on some small pieces of paper. If they have had a bad day, hand them one of your notes to read.
2. If you see a shopping cart or basket loose in the car park or the shop, return it.
3. Don't interrupt when your child is speaking to you.
4. Model saying please and thank you to your child.
5. Model using please and thank you with other people. Your child will notice the way you treat others and will in turn mirror your choices/behaviors.
6. *Give compliments for great service (in stores/ restaurants, etc.) and make a point of asking to speak with a manager to pass compliments about staff/service to them. This models gratitude and appreciation to your child. If you do this often enough, it becomes internalized*

and something that they consider to be "usual," and they are more likely to do the same thing themselves.

7. It's okay to fail, but it doesn't necessarily feel very good. Sometimes failure, or even just the fear of failure, can stop us from doing enjoyable things. So, if your child is worried about losing or getting something wrong, work together to find a list of "famous failures" to remind them not to give up and to keep trying. Some examples you might search for are famous scientists or inventors who made unexpected discoveries, or even athletes who didn't make the cut in certain team sports.

8. Model kindness by being polite to waitstaff, cashiers, and others in service positions.

9. When you are driving, avoid expressing "road rage." Don't swear, tailgate, or make derogatory comments about other drivers around you. Your children are watching and will see this as an appropriate way to manage their anger or even a reaction to fear.

10. Create an email address for your child (keep the address and password a secret). Send them emails to say how proud you are of them, or interesting things you have noticed about them. You could either wait until they are older to give them the password, or you could share your comments now. It's a way of showing your love, affection, and how you notice the little things that they do throughout the day.

11. When driving, show compassion and let someone in when merging, or slow down so someone can cross lanes of traffic. Narrate what you are doing and why you are doing it so your child hears your choice to be kind: "Oh I can see this person

needs to come into our lane. It's pretty busy and I don't think they can find a gap, I should slow down to let them in.'"

12. To spread some holiday cheer, write notes and hide them around your house (this is similar to an Easter egg hunt, or a popular elf Christmas tradition). One note is hidden each day for your child to find with a variety of different themes. Some could include: a fun idea about how to be kind that day, a love note from you (your way of showing them kindness), or it could be the outline/instructions for an activity you could do together. You could pick some of your favorite tips in this book as inspiration.

13. *If you are proud of someone in your life, tell them! Shout it from the rooftops and let your child see you doing it. Not in a false or "set up" way, but explain exactly why you are proud (to the person who is receiving the comments) and let your child see their reaction to your kind words. Afterward, you can even check in with your child and ask them how they think the other person felt when you appreciated their achievements.*

14. Be active together as a family. Okay, so not everyone can run a marathon, but being outside and getting your bodies moving will help to boost everyone's mood through the release of endorphins (feel-good chemicals) and also improve your physical health! Taking care of and making time for ourselves is a way we show "self" kindness.

15. Step out from behind your phone during events! Yes, you might be capturing some beautiful images, but you might miss out on experiencing those moments with your child. Demonstrate to them that you are interested in what they are doing by being physically (and mentally) present.

16. Make it a rule than no one leaves the dinner table until everyone is finished, or they have been given permission to be excused. It demonstrates respect and also protects those fleeting and precious moments of "family time."

17. If your child makes a mistake, forgive them and move on, but do encourage them to think about what they could learn from the mistake. Not in a punitive way, but ask questions like "What would you do differently next time?" This is not only modeling forgiveness, but also teaching problem solving and getting them to consider their behavior and consequences.

18. Show your interest in your child by narrating and reflecting their actions: "I can see how carefully you are coloring." Or "Wow, you were able to do that puzzle so quickly."

19. *It is okay if you express your feelings in front of your child—in fact, I encourage it. Just review the other tips to really ensure that your emotional expression is healthy and adaptive. Being open about how you feel normalizes that feelings are okay, everybody has them, and there is nothing to fear from emotions.*

20. You can either make or purchase some envelopes and stuff love notes or gratitude notes for your child inside. Give your child a stack of sealed envelopes that they can keep safe and open

when they need a little emotional pick-me-up. Expressing love and concern is a great way to model kindness.

21. Model appropriate truth-telling. If they catch you lying, then your kids won't see the need to be honest themselves.

22. Be aware of the tone of your voice. The majority of the message we communicate when talking does not come from the words themselves. So, it's not just what you say, it's how you say it. If there is any discrepancy between the words and other nonverbal cues, people tend to believe or focus on how you said something (rather than the words). So be mindful when praising or disciplining your child, as it might affect the message you are trying to send. Even if you (or your child) are trying to be kind, if your message isn't consistent, then the impact of your kindness might be lost.

23. If your partner, other family members, or even strangers make a mistake, it's important to show forgiveness. You can still have boundaries or express that you have been upset by their action. However, your child is always watching, and this is a great opportunity to model firm boundaries as well as compassion and forgiveness.

24. It is easy to comment on negative things: the stuff that didn't go to plan, mistakes, or other ways that our needs haven't been met. It is important that your child sees a balance, so catch yourself in the act and try and turn it around. Notice and acknowledge neutral and positive things just to create a counterbalance. If you find yourself complaining about traffic, offset it with a comment about how beautiful the weather is, or that fact that you even have a car to drive in (despite the terrible traffic).

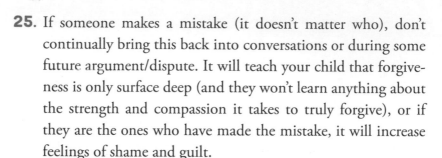

25. If someone makes a mistake (it doesn't matter who), don't continually bring this back into conversations or during some future argument/dispute. It will teach your child that forgiveness is only surface deep (and they won't learn anything about the strength and compassion it takes to truly forgive), or if they are the ones who have made the mistake, it will increase feelings of shame and guilt.

26. If you see someone carrying something heavy or struggling with awkward shopping bags/items, offer to help them. Afterward discuss this with your child. What did it feel like to help? What might the other person have been thinking when you offered to help?

27. Leave little love notes in their lunchbox or school bag for them to find. This models your unconditional love and consideration for them, as well as puts a smile on their face. Let me be honest, though: some older kids might express a bit of embarrassment, but if you create a habit of displaying your love and affection for your child and normalize it, even your teenager will appreciate a love note!

28. Encourage and model strong and appropriate eye contact to demonstrate active listening (which is kind and respectful). Generally, the rule is that the person listening makes more eye contact than the person talking. You can teach them to scan someone's face using a triangle shape: look first at their left eye, then their right eye, then look at their mouth. Then back again. Don't move between them too quickly. It's okay to occasionally look away from the face, and don't forget to blink!

29. Let them see you celebrating and congratulating other people on their successes or achievements (as opposed to judging or being competitive if this was also something you wanted for

yourself). You can demonstrate being upset if you also wanted a prize or particular achievement but not at the expense of others. "I wish I had won that trip away, but I am so glad ____ won. They will have such a lovely time!" They will learn that other's failures aren't linked to their own success or happiness.

30. To help younger children learn about their emotions, sit in front of a mirror together and model different, exaggerated emotional faces; sad, angry, happy, and scared are a good start. Young children love copying and mimicking, so couple this natural behavior with learning opportunities. Make faces and say the emotion that goes with it. See if they can copy your face, and tell them about how to make the face. For example, "This is a sad face. See how my mouth goes down? See if you can make a sad face." Not only are they learning to recognize emotions in other people, but they will also begin to make the connection between the name of an emotion and their own feelings.

31. Be aware of your own self-talk when you make a mistake/error. Your child will hear you and see the way you are processing the issue and will learn that this is how they should treat themselves. You want them to learn that we are all human and all make mistakes—it's completely normal! If you continually beat yourself up for something, or get frustrated with yourself, you can bet your child is watching and internalizing this. Try to reframe your own negative thoughts and ways you talk about mistakes. Use the example/template below to help you openly talk about and accept your own shortcomings: "I was late for work today. I felt so bad because I missed an important meeting, so I apologized to my boss and I will try my best to be on time tomorrow."

32. Show firm boundaries. If you say no, you mean no! This teaches your child to not only respect that others have boundaries, but also models to them that it is also safe for them to have boundaries (which is a protective strategy for their own physical and mental well-being).

33. Self-care part 1. Busy parents still need to look after themselves; in fact, caring for yourself gives you the energy and motivation to be the kind, patient, generous, compassionate parent that you are. If you're running on empty, it's very difficult to be the kind of parent you want to be. So, try to incorporate some self-care into your routine for yourself and your child. Seeing you be kind to yourself also teaches your child about self-worth, and they will mirror or emulate your self-respect.

34. Self-care part 2. Strategies might include maximizing something that you already do in your daily routine, like making a cup of tea/coffee. Incorporate a mindfulness activity that brings you to the present moment (decreasing worried or racing thoughts/worries) while making your hot beverage. Search on the Internet for mindful drinking or mindful scripts to follow when drinking coffee/tea. You could also buy a fancy cup to drink from that makes you smile, or it could be a treat to make yourself a proper coffee (from fresh beans) or tea (from leaves). Encourage your child to join you with their own cup, but only if they are able to sit quietly alongside you. You can talk about the importance of quiet time and how people need to take time out. It can also be important to teach your child boundaries, and that sometimes people need to be alone, so this is an important way to also get them to practice respecting other people's personal boundaries.

35. Self-care part 3. For some of you, exercise is the way you practice self-care, but going to the gym or out for a run by yourself might be too challenging. So, get your child to help you. Set up an obstacle course or circuit that you can follow; for example, a station with a jump rope, a station for burpees, a tunnel to crawl through. Your child will enjoy the sense of pride from putting the activity together with you, and they can also take part in exercise. Self-care is so important, and there are always ways to get creative to ensure it doesn't disappear from your life.

36. *Really listen to your child when they speak—avoid that thing we can do sometimes as parents. "Oh really?" we say, in response to something half heard, or "Hmmm?" which isn't really listening and which we are all guilty of from time to time. Get down on their level, make eye contact, and show you are listening with your entire body (facing them, open body postures, shoulders down, no crossed arms, etc.).*

37. When you are talking with your child, show that you are listening by reflecting or summarizing what they are saying. Not after every sentence, but once they have given you a chunk of information or a complete story, go for it. "Wow, so today in school you had to get up and say your times tables. You said it was really scary, but you did it anyway and got all of them correct. That's great!" It shows them that you have been listening and following and that you are genuinely interested in what they have to say.

38. When you have a conversation with your child, make sure to ask them questions when they tell you something. It will show you are listening and care about their day, hobbies, or interests.

39. Teach them how to show "active listening" by playing a game of sorts. Ask them to tell you a short story and then show what body postures look like when you are not listening (body turned away, arms crossed, no eye contact, not responding to what the other person says) versus active listening (nodding, asking questions, making eye contact). Without saying which is which, ask them which they think showed you were listening and how both examples felt when they were talking. This models not only what active listening looks like but will demonstrate the importance of them being active listeners when other people are talking.

40. *Be on time and encourage them to do so, as well. Discuss why being on time is kind and demonstrates respect to the person waiting for you.*

41. Don't gossip or use judgmental language about others in front of your kids.

42. Be aware of your own attitudes and, more importantly, be honest with yourself here. If you want your children to be tolerant and value diversity, then you need to know what your hidden prejudices are so that you can make efforts to address them. If you don't know what they are, you are at risk of passing along these ideologies to your child.

43. Be mindful of how you talk about people who are different from you. Don't make jokes that use stereotyping. They might seem funny, but they perpetuate stereotypes that are damaging

and show your child that they don't need to demonstrate tolerance or respect for people who are different from them.

44. Create an empathy questionnaire with the following questions and include some lines for your child to put their answers on. Some kids don't like writing, or if this feels too much like homework, give them a bunch of magazines or newspapers that they can cut articles or pictures from to try and answer these questions in another way. If your child is younger, you might modify the questions slightly and ask them or discuss the topics instead of writing.

- What do you think empathy is?
- How do you show empathy?
- When have you shown empathy in the past?
- Why is empathy important?

45. Let them see you struggle. Don't hide your imperfections and faults. Children learn just as much from seeing their parents make a mistake or become frustrated and then fix it in an adaptive and healthy way. It also teaches them self-acceptance and that it's okay that they won't always be good at everything.

46. If you make a choice to be kind in some way, try to narrate your decision-making process with your child. When we share our inner workings, it helps our kids understand why being kind is "worth it." They will come to understand what drives and motivates you to do kind deeds, which in turn helps them internalize these values as their own.

47. *Apologize to your child if you are at fault, or in the wrong. But don't worry—you aren't losing control or admitting defeat. It shows strength and courage*

to apologize when you are in the wrong, which is what you want to teach your child! Get down to their level (body language that shows equal footing and no power or domination), look them in the eye, and use a gentle voice. Say sorry to them and make sure you tell them exactly what behavior/action you are apologizing for.

48. Keep your promises (positive modeling). It demonstrates to your child what respect and integrity look like and you can explain that keeping promises helps build others' trust in your word.

49. Prepare your child's favorite snack or meals, just because! Tell them that you know it's their favorite, and model what it looks like when someone does something randomly kind.

50. Sometimes it is tempting to let your child win every time you play a board game together. But this doesn't give them the skills they need to deal with failure or show them how to maintain relationships with others if some sort of competition is involved (sporting competition, class activities, group games, etc.). Learning to lose graciously is a skill itself, but losing also teaches resilience and gives your child the motivation and ability to pick themselves up and try again. Don't take this away from them! So, play lots of board games with them, tic-tac-toe, running races, and other games where there is a winning and losing situation. Teach them the skills to reframe any negative thoughts or responses to losing:

- It's okay to be upset that you didn't win. I can see that was really important to you.

- You might win next time.
- What skills do you need to learn to be able to win next time?
- Losing that game/race doesn't mean you are no good. You are good at lots of other things. Can you tell me some other things you are good at?
- You could also model what it feels like when you lose a game. Scrunch up your fists and wrinkle your eyebrows "I'm so mad I didn't win! I really wanted to win!" Then start to relax your face, take a few deep breaths, and say something affirming like, "It's okay. I didn't win this time, but I am going to try really hard and win next time." This particular activity takes a little bit of acting skill (in order to keep a straight face), but your child will see your feelings and learn from observation and your "external thoughts" that no one really likes to lose, but we develop self-talk and skills to help us get past the sting of failure.

51. Sometimes kids get so excited that they have won something that they forget what it feels like to be in the opposite situation, they might taunt, tease, or make fun of the other person for losing. So alongside teaching them how to lose, you also need to help your child learn to be a gracious winner. Play lots of games or activities with them that involve a winning and losing situation. If they win, they need to know how to do it without making the other person (intentionally) feel worse. So, you might think about the following ways of supporting them to do this:

    - Name the feelings if they have been taunting or teasing you for losing: "I can see you are really excited that you won, but when you laugh, it makes me feel really sad."

- If you win, model a positive response: "I'm really excited I won, but I am sorry you didn't win that time"
- Talk to them and try and get them to remember what it felt like to lose. Ask them how it felt and what would have made them feel better or worse about the situation. You might prompt them that someone bragging might have made them feel worse.

52. Volunteer at your child's school events. For very busy parents, this can be a really tough one, but find some way to show your interest in your child's world. If you can't make the event itself, send a card to the teacher and class wishing them well, cut up oranges and send them to school for your child to give out at halftime during a sports game, bake for fund-raising drives, etc. Find a way to show interest in their life, because this actively demonstrates and changes the focus of your family from "us" (the family group) to "others" (the wider community), which is important in expanding their circle of concern.

53. *Create a time-out crate for technology and use it at least one day a week. Place all technology (mobiles, tablets, etc.) in the crate, which cannot be accessed. Spend time connecting as a family and being present with one another. This demonstrates care and interest in what others are saying and doing. These things are easier to demonstrate when you aren't stuck in front of technology, as it forces you to engage with one another.*

54. If someone shows you kindness (for example, you drop your wallet and someone chases you down to return it), thank them

but also discuss with your child why you are grateful. "It was kind of that person to return my wallet. They could have taken it, or not bothered to run after me. But they went out of their way to make sure I got it back and I am really grateful." You can even extend this further and ask some questions about how they think you might be feeling, or what made the person return your wallet.

55. At mealtimes, place phones/gaming devices, etc. in the middle of the table. The first one to touch or check their device has to volunteer to do something nice for the other family members.

56. Model smiling at strangers.

57. Sit together and work on writing a list of five things that your child likes about themselves. You can do the activity, too, to model self-love and positive self-esteem. Get them to put their list somewhere they can easily see it to remind themselves of their positives.

58. When we talk, only a small percentage of the message we communicate is through the words we say (generally thought to be somewhere around 7 percent). The remaining part of the message is conveyed by body language and "how" we say the words (tone, volume, speed, pitch, etc.). So, play a game with your child and say the phrase "It's okay" using different emotions as your inspiration and see if they can guess the feeling you are modeling. For example, anger might be narrowed eyes, folded arms, loud voice, while sad might be down turned eyes, slumping posture, and soft or stammering voice. One way that you and your child can demonstrate kindness is by understanding how others might be feeling so that you can support them, so this is an important skill to learn how to identify different feelings and what they look like (even

when someone's words don't match or they try to tell you otherwise!).

59. *Parents, repeat this mantra!* **It's okay to look after yourselves.** *I know sometimes it feels like in order to look after your family, you need to put them first, but if you aren't well (mentally and physically), it makes this task impossible. When your child sees you looking after yourself (through modeling), they learn that it is okay to be kind to themselves. If they see you recognize your value, they will learn to be compassionate to themselves.*

60. Teaching a child to be kind doesn't necessarily mean that, as parents, we have to be passive or give in to them. It's all about learning to follow compassionate learning strategies. You start by reflecting their feelings (or your best guess at what they might be feeling) and then suggest why they might be feeling that way. You then put in a boundary/limit or consequence as appropriate: "I can see you were really angry that I wasn't able to answer your question right away, but I was on the phone. Did you get so angry because I wasn't free to speak when you wanted? (Wait for a response—it's usually an agreement and almost relief that you have understood where they are coming from.) I understand why you got so cross, but I needed to take that call, and it is not okay to interrupt people while they are talking." If this was a more serious issue, or if you already have advised them that a consequence would accompany any interruptions while you are talking on this phone, this is the point where you would gently tell them about the consequence.

61. Smile. Simple, right?! Smile at your child, smile at your family, smile at strangers, and even smile at nothing.

62. Pay attention to the world around you and see opportunities to be kind. Not only for yourself (and the gratification you get), but also for your child to witness. If you see someone struggling with their groceries, or drop a load of items/papers, stop and help them.

63. Make time to read together. For many families, this forms part of a lovely nighttime routine; however, beyond the benefit of shared time together, as your child grows older and they learn to read, ask them to read the bedtime story to you instead. They are developing their skills as well as sharing the role of "caregiver" and nurturing you by reading to you.

64. *Try making some homemade gifts instead of store bought. You might bake some cookies and decorate them as a family, or get your child to think of something they would like to make or create (painting a mug, painting and framing a picture, etc.) to be given to a loved one. You can talk about the appreciation and effort that goes into making presents, rather than simply purchasing them.*

65. Return lost items. If you see a wallet, jacket, or notebook someone has dropped, take it back to them. If you can't see anyone in sight, take it to a shop/store near where you found it and they can hold it as lost property. If the item is a wallet

or is particularly expensive (like a camera or phone), you could even take a trip to the local police station together to report it and hand it in.

66. Show your child affection but with boundaries. Children are usually quite tactile and a hug, stroking their hair, or nurturing is a natural way to demonstrate our love for them. But be aware of your child's personal boundaries, and don't force them to hug or display affection if they aren't comfortable. This teaches them that their personal boundaries deserve to be respected and also gives them positive experiences and knowledge that allows them to understand the need to respect others' personal boundaries.

67. Be prepared! Work through and brainstorm some common frustrations that you and your child experience. Instead of allowing yourselves to react in the heat of the moment, prepare some responses or "scripts" that you can use to manage the situation. Write them up and stick them up where you will all be able to see them so you can remember to use them instead of reacting automatically/negatively.

CHAPTER 3
LANGUAGE

TALK THE TALK

When you speak *with* your child, the language you use is incredibly powerful. Children base their sense of self on the way they are treated by others as well as from the feedback they received about themselves. If the language you use is gentle and reciprocal (the whole reason I said speak *with*, not speak *to*), it helps your child feel secure in their relationship with you. This sense of trust and security allows children to transfer this feeling to other relationships in their lives. Having a strong and secure attachment with you is a good predictor of positive relationships in the future. This comes down to the acceptance and understanding that their needs deserve to be, and will be, met (which makes them happy because they feel fulfilled) and also that other people can be trusted. Children mirror and use the language you use and the way you interact with them as a template for engaging with others. If the language you use is empowering, focused on their strengths, and is compassionate, they will learn how to be kind in the way they speak to others.

Okay then parents, if language is so integral to becoming a compassionate and happy person, let's focus on how to talk the talk.

Children are like sponges, and initially they learn everything from us and their early experiences. This information is then transformed and organized into useable "categories" or mental shortcuts called *schemas*. A schema is useful because it allows us to (almost) instantaneously process vast amounts of information in our environment. Essentially, our mind takes all the information it knows about a subject, topic, object, etc. and applies them to new things being presented to us, e.g., that thing is small, brown, furry with a wagging tail, so it must be a dog. We also develop schemas about ourselves: Who do we think we are? What do we expect from ourselves? How do we expect to be treated?

The issue with schemas is that once we have collected enough information about something, our thought process becomes relatively automatic, so we are prone to finding information or data that supports our current beliefs or expectations. In essence, we want to create early experiences for our children that support the development of positive schemas about themselves and others, because once a negative schema has been developed, it can become challenging to address or change. These schemas will also impact how your child responds to and treats others, as well as themselves. This may influence their ability to demonstrate kindness, as it can be challenging for

Key Definitions

Self-efficacy—a person's belief that they are capable of achievement or meeting certain goals.

them to interact in a gentle or empathetic way if their automatic thoughts are negative or pessimistic.

I have worked with many adults and children who hold a negative view of themselves; it can impact their self-esteem, **self-efficacy**, relationships, and attitudes toward others. One example I recall vividly involves an eight-year-old boy I worked with. This young boy had been told he wasn't very good at reading by a number of different people. His peers made fun of him when he was selected to read aloud in the class, and his teacher became frustrated with him due to challenging behaviors he exhibited to get out of activities that involved reading (being a class clown, defiance, absconding from the classroom, etc.). He heard these messages enough times that he internalized this into his schema and developed a belief that he was terrible at reading. After being diagnosed with dyslexia and receiving support, his reading improved; however, he still could not get his thoughts to shift from his original schema that made him believe he was no good at reading. Even though he was quite a proficient reader, he still felt nervous when having to read aloud and became quite disruptive when asked to do any classroom task that involved reading (tests, workbooks, etc.), and these behaviors negatively impacted his school results.

The way that we treat others and ourselves and the language we use are absorbed by our children. So, we want to fill them up with positive and compassionate thoughts and expectations as opposed to negative or possibly judgmental ideas. In particular, we can use language to our advantage to help our children become kind people. Words have power and can build us up or tear us down, so we need to teach our children to harness the power of language to help them prepare for the inevitable challenges that they will face in life. Specifically, kindness can be influenced by the way you as a parent *speak to* your child(ren), the type of the language you use to describe or *talk about* your children (and others), as well as the way you model and encourage positive *self-talk* for your child. This chapter will cover four key areas that will give your child the gift of kindness through language and communication:

- How you talk to your child
- The power of words
- How you talk about others
- Teaching self-talk

HOW YOU TALK TO YOUR CHILD

Similar to the chapter on modeling, the most effective way to get your child to speak kindly to others is by demonstrating to them exactly what you expect. This might be uncomfortable, but spend some time reflecting on the way you speak to your child. Do you speak harshly? Do you use manners when you interact? How do you show them you are displeased? Do you raise your voice? It might not always be a pretty picture. You may feel tired, over-whelmed, and irritated at times, leading you to respond curtly or abruptly. This may be the case and we can easily excuse our own behavior; however, we often ask more of our children than we ask of ourselves. Adults often accept or acknowledge that having a bad day or "waking up on the wrong side of the bed" can result in frayed tempers, irritation, the odd bout of yelling. Yet, there is also this expectation that children should somehow be kind, respectful, and manage their emotions in all circumstances—even though, as adults, we are acutely aware that some days just get the better of us. I'm not saying that either you or your child should or could be perfect, but just be aware of the consistency in the messages you give to your child about speaking and acting kindly.

Think about how you would like your child to speak to you or others and try and model those expectations. Consider the way you speak to them, and use your tone and manner to show them (rather than telling them) what your expectations are. This can be really tough, especially if your child is misbehaving or you are feeling overwhelmed/tired/irritated. And I won't pretend I am a perfect person or mother; I, too, have moments where I want to tear my hair out. But these are the moments where the real lessons are learned, where your child sees how you are able to remain kind, gentle, and respectful even when you are frustrated. The following chapter contains some clear tips you can use to practice this skill and activities that can help you introduce this idea to your children. However, there are a few important ground rules to help you understand these activities:

- Think about the tone of your voice. The majority of the message you communicate to others is nonverbal (including the tone, pitch, and volume of your voice). If you are mad, irritated, or frustrated, really focus on dropping the volume and speed of your voice and speaking softly and slowly. This will help you communicate your message clearly.
- Think about the language you use. Try not to shame your child if they have made a mistake or misbehaved. Use respectful language to communicate the issue or error and name the *behavior* as being unacceptable, not your child. If you use language like "You are so bad! I can't believe you did

that!" your child internalizes they are bad, which can lead to a negative self-belief. This, in turn, can lead to a self-fulfilling prophecy, where they expect or truly believe that they are bad, so they "do bad things." Focus instead on the behavior or action itself; "I don't like you" versus "I don't like that behavior" is a very important distinction to make.

- Limit the number of criticisms you have. Yes, they might have left a wet towel on their bedroom floor for the hundredth time that week, or forgotten to put their cereal bowl in the sink *again*, but too much criticism can leave your child feeling low, unskilled, worthless, and less willing to try again in the future.

Please know that it is okay not to be perfect all the time. You might have some days where you do snap, or use language that you don't necessarily like, but if you can focus on these tips, it will give your child the opportunity to witness respectful and gentle communication. You can also own up to your mistakes to show your child that being human is okay and that taking responsibility for your actions is important. They learn from the way you interact with them, including using your actions and words as templates that they apply to the relationships and interactions they have with other people. Although I will shortly explore some key ways we can shape their language, know that the first step to teaching them to use kind words is for them to know what it feels like to be on the receiving end of them.

THE POWER OF WORDS

Kindness is not only modeled by the way you speak to your child, but it can also be impacted by the words you teach and language you encourage. If your child can use appropriate, polite, and respectful language to talk about, and with, other people in their world, it will maximize their opportunities to develop and maintain relationships, share information, and get their needs met. All of these are key to positive mental health and happiness. If you encourage the use of kind language, it is another avenue through which your child can demonstrate compassion, respect, and genuine care for the people around them.

Manners

Using manners is one way that we show compassion and respect, but it is also a behavior that is necessary for humans in order to coexist harmoniously. It shows a sense of acknowledgment and appreciation for the roles we each play, which allows us to have a life that runs smoothly . . . well, most of the time anyway. Spend a minute or two thinking about the different people in your life who impact your day; immediate and extended family, friends, colleagues, the barista who makes your coffee in the morning, other drivers on the road, etc. If everybody just did what they wanted, then anarchy would reign. People are generally courteous and follow the rules, but we just forget to notice it and can certainly forget to acknowledge when someone lets us merge or makes us the perfect latte in the morning to really get our day started right. So, take the time to appreciate these other people who play a part in your life, even if they are simply following a certain set of rules or social expectations. And let your child see you using manners and acknowledging the presence and actions of others.

Start introducing manners into your child's vocabulary very early on. Encourage your child to use *please* and *thank you* in social situations and within the home. You can do this by modeling manners yourself (when you speak to your child, and when you speak to other people) and as they get older, you can have more direct conversations about when to use manners and why they are so important. Initially, your child will simply learn to use them when someone gives something to them (thanks for sharing your cake with me) or when they want something (please can I have some juice); however, as they get older, they will need to learn about the appreciation that underpins both. When you teach your child to say thank you, you are teaching them to show appreciation and gratitude for something they have been given. This demonstration of appreciation goes a long way toward building fulfilling relationships and helping others feel good (pretty much kindness in a nutshell). When they learn about saying please, it is a way of asking for help. Sometimes people feel vulnerable about asking for help, but try to encourage them that it is okay to do so. Using "please" is also going to help them have their needs met, as people are more likely to lend a hand if they are asked politely.

Is Honesty Always the Best Policy?

Why does it seem like our children don't always tell the truth when they should ("I didn't eat that piece of cake," said the child with suspicious chocolate icing around their mouth) versus when it might be more appropriate to keep the truth to themselves ("Mommy, I think your hat looks weird!"). I'm sure you've heard the old saying "If you can't say anything nice, then don't say anything at all." Most would agree that this is a good saying that helps teach your children about the impact of their language and encourages them to monitor or modulate the way they interact with others. While I like that element of the saying, I also disagree with it, as I think there's more nuance required than "only say nice things out loud." In some circumstances, honesty is needed and is a kinder, but infinitely more difficult, thing to share. It's a fine balance between being honest versus ensuring that your child is still courteous and respectful. Because they are still adjusting and finetuning their filters, children need help learning how to make this distinction.

If you want an honest answer to something . . . just ask a child, but be prepared for the unfiltered, brutal, and often hilarious responses that come barreling out of their angelic little mouths. But is the brutality of truth or lying worse? I think there is absolutely a middle ground, which I will explore shortly; however, it is important to outline the complex concept of lying first. And both lying and being honest, along with how they are delivered, can directly influence whether someone is perceived as kind or compassionate.

The ability to lie evolves as part of a normal developmental stage and tends to start around age three or four when children learn to recognize what is real and what is make-believe. Before this time, children aren't really lying; they are just mixing up reality, thoughts, and imagination. Lying actually takes a lot of skill and is an adaptive social skill that starts with little experiments to gauge the reaction of others. The purpose of lying tends to fit into the following categories:

- Testing or practicing, which is all about trialing lying in general to see what other people believe and where certain boundaries are, i.e. who can I lie to and what kind of lies can I get away with?
- Making themselves feel more important or fit in, in a similar way to keeping up with the Joneses. It is usually to get some

41

kind of positive feedback about themselves that boosts their self-esteem and need for attention.

- Telling a lie to protect someone else, including another person's feelings. This is quite an adaptive social tool usually used to protect relationships.
- Probably the most serious of the lies is one told to avoid punishment or negative consequences for a wrongdoing. If children are rewarded for lying (they get away with it), or are allowed to lie, this behavior is likely to persist into adulthood.

We cannot expect our children to be "perfect" all the time; however, we do need to help them develop a filter, because although honesty is the best policy, they need to know how to be honest without being hurtful. We also don't want to accidentally reinforce lying. So how can you find the middle ground? Essentially, it's about teaching your child how to deliver the truth in a gentle way. This skill is particularly important in being able to demonstrate kindness, as it shows empathy and compassion for another's feelings but also protects them from the damage of a lie. For example, your child's best friend asks them whether they like their new T-shirt, and your child doesn't like it, so it is important to explore how they might choose to respond. Children work well with concrete examples, steps, and strategies to help them navigate "social waters." They need to plan ahead and think about how they will respond to certain scenarios: Will they be honest? What might be the impact of their honesty on their friend or friendship? Is there any way they could find something positive about the T-shirt? Examples you could use to help them with this potentially awkward question and answer about the T-shirt include:

- "Do you like it?"—if your child really cannot find anything they like about something, they can instead turn the question back around and find out what their friend thinks.
- "I really like the color!"—find something about the T-shirt that they do like and highlight that.
- "I like how you matched it with your jeans"—highlighting something else they like that is related to the T-shirt, without having to directly compliment the T-shirt itself.

However, it is also important to acknowledge that in certain situations telling the truth in a helpful way might be what the other person needs the most and is actually an act of kindness. Receiving accurate feedback in a loving and caring way is an important part of a trusted relationship. The courage to give and receive truthful feedback is a key component of growth and flexible thinking. There are a few ways you can teach your child to be honest (when appropriate) and tactful when managing a challenging situation. These specific tips follow in the next chapter.

AGREE TO DISAGREE!

It is a normal stage of development when young children (generally toddler age) start hitting when they are upset, and in later years, physicality (or using their physical strength to get their way, shoving, hitting, kicking, etc.) might arise due to peer pressure or even be exacerbated by hormonal fluctuations. Although we might understand why it occurs, this doesn't mean that, in either case, physical harm is acceptable. Teaching your child how to use their words instead of being aggressive to get their way is a key stage of their development. If you can encourage them to be able to manage intense feelings and use their words to express themselves (instead of their fists, or rude/mean words), it will go a long way toward being able to demonstrate kindness toward others, even during times of stress for themselves. There is an entire chapter later in the book dedicated to emotional regulation, but this particular discussion focuses on how your child can still try and get their needs met by using their words.

- **Redirection**—identify the issue and gently remind them of the appropriate or expected way they should interact with others. Particularly for younger children, just keep it simple! "Remember that we need to take turns with our toys." Children can be quite impulsive and can easily be influenced or distracted, so once you have given a verbal cue or reminder, you can then redirect them to another quieter activity or to a new area away from whatever triggered their big feelings. "Come on over here and help me with this puzzle."
- **Independence**—children use their words to assert their independence and gain attention, and will often use language to see what they can get away with. Kids usually say rude words or other hurtful things to try and have their needs met in some way. I'm not saying this is particularly helpful or appropriate, but they don't have the language skills yet to do it any other way. Try to figure out what they need or want, talk them through it, and give them language to express themselves in more appropriate ways.
- **Feelings**—similar to the previous point, children use their words to express their feelings. If they are frustrated, sad, or scared, their language will reflect this. When encouraging

your child to be kind, it is key to give them words so that they can express their feelings appropriately. For example, it's okay for them to say no if they don't want to play with someone, but give them examples of how they can do this in a kind and considerate way: "I'm sorry, I don't want to play that game" versus "Go away! I don't want to play with you" will have very different outcomes.

- **Questions**—use real-life examples, favorite books, and TV shows, etc. for learning opportunities. If you see someone being mean or rude, ask your child what they think: "Why do you think that person was using mean words?" "How do you think it made the other person feel?" etc. Children use their own experiences and feelings when they try to put themselves in someone else's shoes. So, their answers will give you a lot of really valuable information about your child's feelings and thoughts. It will also start building their empathy, as they will begin to take notice of how other people might feel.

- **Prevention**—you can also help your child come up with a mental list of questions to ask themselves to prevent future outbursts. However, if I am being honest, it's not always entirely preventable, but giving your child appropriate ways of managing big feelings or reacting to stressful situations will help them make better choices. Try and encourage them to engage the "thinking" part of their brain, rather than the reactive part. Come up with a list of questions they can ask themselves if they get into tricky situations or feel overwhelmed and think about possible consequences for different choices.

HOW WE TALK ABOUT OTHERS

It's not just about giving our children the right language tools; we also need to show them how to communicate with others. Modeling kind and compassionate language is powerful, and our children are finely tuned to learn, and if we expect them to be kind, we need to show them using our actions and our words. They will pick up on any inconsistencies in what you ask of them, yet don't demonstrate yourself. There is something horrifying for parents when they hear their own phrases being parroted back to them, and I don't mean their gentle and empathetic phrases—I mean the accidental ones, or the automatic ones that just slip out. For example, a client's mother arrived at our session one day in tears. They were driving to the session, and a car had pulled out in front of their car without indicating, so the mother tooted the horn and her little girl piped up from the back of the car: "Were they driving like a d*ckhead, mum?" The mother was horrified because she heard her own language being parroted back to her and knew immediately that her daughter had picked it up from her.

You can't pick and choose what your child will copy; in fact, they are probably going to hold more gleefully on to your faux pas or slipups rather than perfectly mimicking you saying, "Thank you for passing the gravy, I really appreciate it." It is hard to be consistent all the time, and as a parent, you can't be expected to be perfect; however, it is important to think about the content of what you say and the language you use. This awareness will help you to make decisions about what it is you want your child to hear. If you are aware of something, you can either stop or adjust it. If you aren't aware of your behaviors, then how can you make changes? So, what are your standard responses that just pop out in a frustrated moment? Try and reflect on your most common ones, think about the potential impact of your child hearing them, and don't be shy or judgmental of yourself if you do pick any up. It's important to figure this stuff out, even if it feels uncomfortable, because if you aren't aware of your automatic language/responses, then you cannot make any changes, and these are likely to be habits that your child will pick up on.

TEACHING POSITIVE SELF-TALK

It's important to understand that it is not enough just to teach your child to be kind to others. For them to truly demonstrate kindness, they need to know it's not just about being kind on the surface. It's about the sense of fulfilment they experience by genuinely being a kind person. Kindness is not just about being nice to other people, but it also extends to ourselves. Self-talk is the way you talk to yourself, or your inner voice. Positive and negative self-talk can be linked to a child's schema or beliefs about themselves. A child might think "I'm stupid" or "I'm useless," which are two examples of negative self-talk. Now just imagine how these thoughts would make a child feel.

If a person experiences negative self-talk, it will generally lead to feeling low or flat and possibly impact their self-esteem. The opposite is generally true for positive self-talk. It's not only thoughts about ourselves; we also have a running commentary in our minds about others (individuals, groups, or communities of people). Our self-talk can be positive, negative, or neutral, but it will directly impact how we treat people and how we expect them to treat us. Those who think and process things in a compassionate and optimistic way are more likely to have better self-esteem, higher motivation, and increased ability to regulate their emotions. These higher levels of positive automatic thoughts are correlated with increased levels of happiness.

Self-talk is a really important component of kindness, as it reflects the expectations we have for ourselves and others, and we want to foster a caring, gentle, and empathetic voice in our children. The good thing is that you can help your child address and retrain negative self-talk if you recognize that it is happening. I have provided specific tips and activities you can implement to do this, but in general, there are a number of effective ways you can address negative, automatic thoughts. First, you need to identify that these potentially negative thoughts exist and find out what they are. How can you fix something if you don't know what the exact issue is? Second, we model positive self-talk, and third, we create opportunities to counteract negative thoughts and create opportunities to practice a more adaptive, healthy, and positive response to these thoughts. Developing a compassionate inner voice helps your child become kind to not only other people, but themselves, as well.

REFLECTION EXERCISES—TALKING THE TALK

1. Think about the schemas you have made for yourself, and your immediate family (including your child). What are the thoughts, expectations, and assumptions you have about yourself and others?

2. Do you think these schemas are helpful or a hindrance?

3. How do you speak to your child? Think about your tone, the words you use, and the attitudes that you convey when you speak.

4. How do you talk to other people? Are you consistent in what you offer when you communicate with a wide range of people? (i.e., compassionate, kind, respectful).

5. In moments of frustration, what are your go-to phrases or words? Thinking about what you have learned so far in the book, what do you think you could change those words/phrases to be instead?

CHAPTER 4
TIPS FOR LANGUAGE

◇◇

68. Encourage them to learn people's names and use them in conversation.

69. Ask them what they think kindness looks like? (Focusing on behaviors).

70. Ask them to explain the difference between kind and unkind thoughts.

71. Ask them how they feel when someone has been kind to them.

72. Ask them how they feel when they have been kind to someone.

73. Ask them how they feel when someone has been unkind to them. These particular questions get them reflecting and translating their own experiences onto others (the first step in developing empathy—being able to see/feel things from another person's perspective).

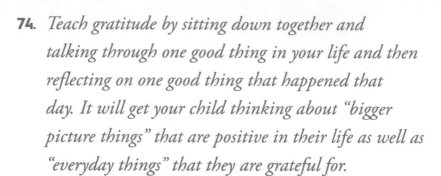

74. *Teach gratitude by sitting down together and talking through one good thing in your life and then reflecting on one good thing that happened that day. It will get your child thinking about "bigger picture things" that are positive in their life as well as "everyday things" that they are grateful for.*

75. Teach your child how to reflect emotions to show other people they are listening and care about what someone is experiencing. Some good templates are:
- "It sounds like that made you really (insert emotion word)."
- "Wow, you were so (insert emotion word)."
- "I bet that made you feel (insert emotion word)."

76. Set up an activity about crying babies that can work for older and younger children. Essentially, you want to get them thinking empathetically, but also reflecting on their own individual ways of seeking help and expressing their feelings. Ask them the following questions:
- "Why do babies cry?" You can give them some education/information if they struggle with this question. Essentially, you want them to identify that this is how babies communicate since they don't have the words to tell people what they need.
- Next ask them the following question "If babies can't speak about their feelings, but bigger kids can, what are some of the ways that you do this? How do you tell us what you feel?" You might encourage them to think

about words they use or their actions that communicate their feelings to you.

77. When you talk about the hopes and wishes you have for your children, focus your intentions on kindness. So instead of saying something like "I just want you to be happy," or "I want you to be successful," try to emphasize kindness instead. "I want you to be kind," or "I just want you to be a good person."

78. If you see that a family member or friend is upset, try to reflect the feeling that you notice and offer them support (this only works if your child also happens to be around for the vicarious learning opportunity). You might say something like, "It seems like you are really sad. Is there anything I can do to help?" Depending on the age of your child, you might also extend this by having a discussion later and asking them how the person might have felt when you acknowledged their feelings and offered to do something to help them.

79. If you see a family member or friend who is upset, you might use the opportunity to explore and build empathy within your child. "Your cousin was feeling really cross today because he wanted to get up from the dinner table and play. But he hadn't finished eating his food yet." It gets them thinking about their own feelings (*yeah, I would feel pretty frustrated, too*) and also understanding that other people can have emotional responses to things.

80. *Avoid having the TV on during dinner. It stops potential discussions and connection between family members, but it also stops you from really listening and paying attention to your child and other family members if you're distracted by a TV show.*

81. Reframe negative thoughts. If they are asking questions like "Why me?" or "Why does bad stuff happen to me?" help them reframe and think about what a situation is teaching them. Are they going to learn a new skill to get rid of the problem? Will they learn how much of a fighter they are? Or how strong they are? Instead of thinking about what they lack, help them learn to be kind to themselves and think about themselves in a more positive light. This helps promote a positive internal voice.

82. Be aware of the volume of your voice, especially if you're feeling frustrated. Shouting might attract someone's attention, but it doesn't help you communicate your needs or get people to listen to your words. Model the power of a quiet and calm voice in getting your point across. This will also teach your child that despite feeling frustrated, it's important to be respectful to others and use kind words. You can also get them to think about the nonverbal messages that people might pick up if you are yelling, rather than speaking.

83. Teach them how to offer a "constructive criticism sandwich"—being honest still requires respect and general courtesy, which makes this a good strategy to use. The criticism is in the middle, sandwiched between two positive statements. "I can see you tried your best during the game, you got a bit distracted in the middle, but then pulled it together and scored a goal!"

84. Create a Complaints Penalty Jar. Think about this in a similar way that you would a swear jar. Set your family a challenge for one week. Each person starts with a certain amount of coins in a jar (only a small amount). If anyone complains, then a coin is deducted and put in the Penalty Jar. At the end of the

week, any money in the penalty jar is donated and any money left in personal jars is given to that person. You could extend this and make it a month, but this will depend on the concentration ability of your child. You could also do this activity with tokens instead of coins, and the tokens can be traded for objects, activities, experiences, sweets, time spent watching their favorite movie, a family trip to the museum, etc.

85. Work on a collage together (print out pictures from the Internet, or cut out pictures from magazines/newspapers) to promote positive self-talk. Create a theme like "I am . . ." and get them to fill in the blank (brave, happy, smart, caring, etc.) and then find images that match this idea. Create a collage with their message and display it proudly.

86. *Create a wall chart with examples of positive self-talk or affirming statements and place it next to the bathroom mirror where they can see it every morning and night.*

87. Find child-appropriate ways to explain things so that you can avoid lying if they ask awkward questions. Children are particularly open about discussing different physical appearances. If your child asks you about someone who wears different clothes than you, speaks a different language, has a different ability, or is different in any physical way, you could start by asking questions to see how much they already understand. In addition, you could work together and do some research on the Internet to find out some more information (just have a quick pre-read to ensure the topics are age- and developmentally appropriate).

88. While honesty is important, children need to learn how to filter their questions and comments. Get them to ask these questions to themselves before they make any comments or answer questions when they need to be honest. These questions can help them figure out whether their questions are kind.

- Is it true?
- Is it kind?
- Is it necessary?

89. Sometimes we accidentally encourage little white lies in order to be socially appropriate, but this is just confusing for children. So, it is more appropriate to teach them to soften the truth by focusing on a positive aspect or element of something or by asking questions. An example might be a friend asking if your child likes their new top (hint: your child doesn't like it). You might encourage your child to tell your friend what they do like about it ("I really like the colors") or ask questions ("Where did you get your new top?"). It still shows interest and compassion without necessarily needing to lie.

90. If you hear your child say something like "I only won because of luck!" or another statement that an achievement was not due to their own efforts, then pick this statement apart with them. Thinking like this doesn't acknowledge their skills or perseverance, and they will most likely feel devalued. Sit down and find out what they needed to do to win and help them to see, acknowledge, and appreciate their attributes.

91. *Instead of asking your child if they had a good day, get more specific. Ask them: "Did anything disappoint you today?" and "What was the best thing that*

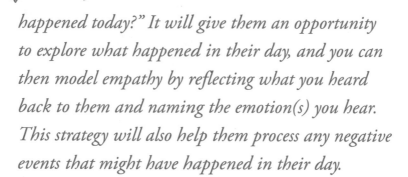

happened today?" It will give them an opportunity to explore what happened in their day, and you can then model empathy by reflecting what you heard back to them and naming the emotion(s) you hear. This strategy will also help them process any negative events that might have happened in their day.

92. Stop gossip. If your child is old enough, then you can use the Whispers Game, or Telephone, as an example of how the truth can get twisted when people pass along messages or gossip. The game involves sitting in a circle. One person starts by whispering a statement in the ear of the person next to them and is not allowed to repeat themselves. The person who heard the whisper then passes along the message to the next person. When the message gets back to the person who started, they call out what they heard and tell everyone if there was any difference between the original and final statements. It can be amusing to hear just how much changed, but it also shows your child how messages can get mixed up.

93. You can start a discussion with your child about how it might feel to be the person being gossiped about. Ask questions to try and figure out why it might not feel very good to have rumors spread about them. This will help them develop empathy, and they will be less likely to gossip themselves if they truly understand the emotional impact rumors can have on people.

94. Each day after school, ask them to identify the two best things and the (one) worst thing that happened during the day. This

is useful for children and adolescents, as it avoids the trap of "yes/no" answers and develops their ability to self-reflect on their emotional experiences. It also gives you a chance to check in around their emotional needs or anything that might have come up for them during the day.

95. *Reflect and name their feelings when you see them: "Gee, it sounds like you are really sad" or "Wow, that seems like it made you feel angry." It will help younger children identify their feelings, and it also helps demonstrate to children of all ages that you care about and are interested in their experiences.*

96. Name your own emotions when you experience them. This is good modeling, it promotes open and honest communication, and also teaches them empathy (as they can reflect and understand that others also have emotions and responses to situations/events).

97. Model how to have a good argument. Show them how to navigate a fight with compassion and strong boundaries for themselves. Teach them to focus on their own feelings (not what the other person has done, as this can feel like blaming and shaming to the other person, and will nearly always mean a bigger fight), take responsibility for their actions, and encourage them to try and see things from the other person's point of view. This sounds like a lot, and without lecturing them, the best way you can do this is by demonstrating how you do it.

98. If you celebrate Thanksgiving, take your family for a walk and collect some fallen leaves. Glue the leaves to a thick piece of cardboard and write what you are thankful for on each leaf. You can then display your art over your dinner table. If you don't celebrate Thanksgiving, you can still collect leaves in autumn and create a masterpiece of gratitude.

99. Be very clear and label kindness when you see kindness in the world. Don't shy away from shouting this kind of behavior from the rooftops for all to hear. When you notice and acknowledge kindness, it strengthens and encourages your child to see the value in it. So, when you see someone being thoughtful, considerate, or empathetic, have a discussion with your child: "Did you see that person being really kind to their friend? What did you notice them doing? Why do you think they did it? What would it be like to be their friend (who received the kindness)?"

100. *Try to avoid using generic comments like "good boy" or "good girl" to try and promote kindness and compassion. First, you want to label specific kind behaviors, and second, you want to avoid your child potentially feeling ashamed if they aren't always able to be kind/empathetic, etc. or fearing the opposite (being a bad/naughty boy or girl).*

101. If you hear them say words like "You're wrong" to someone else, help them try and figure out another, kinder, way that they can get their point across. Ask them for suggestions of how they might do this, or give them some examples if they

are struggling: "I'm not really sure about that. Can I check with someone else?" "I'm sorry but I think differently, and that's okay if we disagree," or "I learned something different. Can I share it with you?"

102. If you hear your child having a disagreement with someone, you can either gently step in and try to facilitate/negotiate a good outcome, or speak to them afterward about how they could repair any ruptures to the relationship. First, ask them their opinion and what they think they could do next to try and fix the situation. If they have trouble, you could suggest apologizing, recognizing where the situation went wrong, or possibly doing something kind to show they care about the person they argued with.

103. Play a game with them and set out scenarios, for example: "Ash needed to say some lines in the school play, but before she got on stage, she was really nervous." Then get them to give you an example of a negative self-talk statement (e.g., "Everyone will laugh because I will make a mistake") and a positive self-talk statement (e.g., "I'm nervous, but I have practiced really hard at getting my lines right"). Ask them how "Ash" might feel if she experienced either the positive or negative self-talk. This game is all about learning the impact of negative self-talk as well as practicing self-kindness to positively impact mood and self-confidence.

104. Teach them how to disagree respectfully, part 1. It is okay to disagree, and it's important for their own sense of well-being and safety that they know it's acceptable to disagree or have different opinions. Just help them learn how to do it in a respectful way. First, help them not to make their disagreement personal: ensure that they tell the other person that they

don't like the idea, but it has nothing to do with the other person.

105. Teach them how to disagree respectfully, part 2. Help them practice "I" statements, because "You" statements can come across as argumentative. For example, "*You* always make me feel angry when *you* ask me to do my chores over and over. I know that I have to do them" versus "*I* understand I need to do my chores, but *I* feel upset being asked to do them again." Using "I" instead of "You" takes ownership and responsibility

106. Teach them how to disagree respectfully, part 3. Even though they might not agree, try to get your child to listen to the other person's perspective or argument. Simply by actively listening (not necessarily agreeing), they are protecting the relationship with the other person by acknowledging their point of view and showing respect by understanding that there are many other opinions on a topic.

107. Teach them how to disagree respectfully, part 4. Remain calm and let them know that they can move away from a situation they don't want to be in! Get them to use whatever strategy works best for them (see the chapter and tips on Emotional Regulation in this book and figure out which one your child prefers, page 85). If they can remain calm, they are less likely to become aggressive or argumentative, which may potentially damage a relationship or get them in trouble.

108. Read with your child. Depending on their age, you can read picture books, short stories, newspaper articles, magazine articles, novels, etc. The important thing is to pick a story that has characters in it (fiction or nonfiction is fine), not a story that focuses on an event. As you read, they begin understanding and deciphering the characters' intentions,

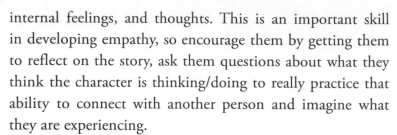

internal feelings, and thoughts. This is an important skill in developing empathy, so encourage them by getting them to reflect on the story, ask them questions about what they think the character is thinking/doing to really practice that ability to connect with another person and imagine what they are experiencing.

109. Help your child learn about the importance of their voice when communicating, part 1. You can help them by playing a game where you say the same sentence with different emphasis on different words and see if it changes the meaning. Get them to guess or discuss what they think changes in your message:

- *I* wasn't lying (implies it was someone else).
- I *wasn't* lying (implies that they were not lying).
- I wasn't *lying* (gives the impression that they were doing something other than lying).

110. Help your child learn about the importance of their voice when communicating, part 2. Play a game where you practice saying the same sentence but with a different pitch/tone/volume to see if it changes the meaning. Ask them what they think about each sentence and what you mean:

- That is so interesting (use an excited, higher pitched voice) *versus* That is so interesting (use a flat monotone voice and maybe an eye roll)
- I had a really good day (sniffle, hiccup, quiet and slow voice) *versus* I had a really good day (loud, cross, fast speech)

111. Every night when you have dinner, carve out a few minutes to talk (as a family) about any kindness you noticed that day. It makes kindness part of your daily world, and noticing or

being aware of kindness can actually increase the desire to be kind yourself.

112. Remove "Don't" from the language you use with your child. Using this word too often can be quite negative, as it leaves children feeling like they are already in trouble before they have done anything wrong when actually we only want to give a warning or set a boundary. Try and replace some of your "don'ts."

    - Don't run → Please walk
    - Don't fall off → Try and be careful
    - Don't interrupt when people are talking → Let other people finish talking first
    - Don't throw things → Could you try to put them down carefully?

113. When teaching positive self-talk, you can help your child by teaching them about Yes People and No People. Not necessarily people who say yes and no, but more that Yes People have a positive mind-set (I can do this!) versus No People (I can't do this!) who have a negative or pessimistic mind-set. Ask your child which one they think they are.

114. To extend the previous activity, work with your child to figure out what makes a Yes or No Person. What do they do differently? How do you think being a Yes or No person would change their experiences?

115. *Implement a weekly (or possibly biweekly) family meeting. During this meeting, you could have a fixed agenda, or you could take turns talking through good things and challenges that have occurred throughout*

the week. This is where you can work on conflict or negotiate upcoming events/activities. It gives children the opportunity to be included in family decisions, but also gives them space to be heard and practice listening to others.

116. Introduce a "talking" object. This object can be used during family meetings or important discussions, or can be grabbed at any time if someone really wants the other people in your family to listen. When someone has the talking object (which could be a teddy bear, trophy, pretend microphone, anything really) then everyone else has to listen. You might add some rules, like a maximum time limit that someone can have hold of the item. But essentially you are wanting to create opportunities for your child to feel heard, but also respect and accept when another person wants to be heard.

117. Come up with a family motto. Figure out what you stand for as a family and what you are striving toward. You can have some fun and create a family crest or emblem, as well. It opens up discussions about what everyone in the family wants from each other and also what you expect from each other. The motto could focus on respect, empathy, caring, or any other element that you all feel passionately about or deem to be important to your family.

118. Teach them the following phrases to help them express their feelings when someone has upset them. It's important to own their feelings and focus on how something has affected them (but still try to avoid shaming the other person).

- I feel (insert feeling word like: *sad, frustrated, worried,* etc.) . . . when you (insert whatever behavior/action has upset them) . . . because (insert why they have felt this way).
- E.g., "I feel sad when you don't listen to me because I feel like I am not important."

119. Practice a daily ritual and get in the habit of expressing gratitude in your family. Try for at least one comment for each family member to let them know why you appreciate them.

120. Give your child a new pen and notebook so that they can start a gratitude journal. For younger kids, you can make this part of your night time routine and fill the journal in together. Take a few minutes each day to reflect on the things you are grateful for. It doesn't have to be big or grand, just the simple things that you appreciate. If you aren't sure where to start, take a look at the resources at the back of this book to help you prepare for a monthlong gratitude challenge—with a new prompt for each day to help you and your child reflect.

121. *Don't talk about your child negatively in front of them. I know that sometimes as parents you can be frustrated when your child isn't following the rules, but save any comments for a more private time when your child cannot overhear you. The words that you speak, and the way that you talk about your child, helps form their opinion of themselves . . . so focus on giving them positive examples.*

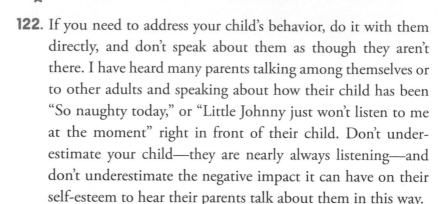

122. If you need to address your child's behavior, do it with them directly, and don't speak about them as though they aren't there. I have heard many parents talking among themselves or to other adults and speaking about how their child has been "So naughty today," or "Little Johnny just won't listen to me at the moment" right in front of their child. Don't underestimate your child—they are nearly always listening—and don't underestimate the negative impact it can have on their self-esteem to hear their parents talk about them in this way.

123. If you hear your child saying words and phrases like "I am no good at this," try to help them reframe their thoughts. Ask them to try and think about it another way: "I can hear what you are saying, so let's think together. What would you need to learn or practice to get better?" or "It's hard when we aren't good at everything, but tell me, what are some of the things you are good at?" Get them to change their focus from the negatives to how they could take ownership and improve or reflect on things that they are good at instead.

124. If you hear your child using negative self-talk, you could ask them about how having negative thoughts, or saying negative things about themselves, impacts their mood and self-belief. Ask them what would happen if they believed these thoughts (hint: it might be low mood, low self-confidence, and not wanting to try things or miss out on potentially exciting things because they think they might fail or be embarrassed if they can't do something). For younger children, you might simplify this and talk about how these kinds of thoughts can make us feel yukky, and you might need to prompt or remind them about persistence and trying again. You can help them

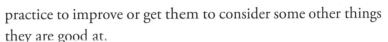

practice to improve or get them to consider some other things they are good at.

125. If you hear your child saying something like "It's too hard," try to help them think about the situation another way. You might get them to repeat positive phrases like "This is going to take some more practice." Or you can help them understand that they might not get things right the first time around or that it is okay to ask for help.

126. If you, your child, or anyone else in your family/friendship group makes a mistake, let them know that it is okay. You can use statements like "I know that was an accident" or "That's all right, it was just an accident." You want to focus on labeling the action, not the person.

127. Arrange a "family meeting" and explore what everyone in your household thinks your "family values" are. Discuss what everyone thinks that the family unit wants to work toward, how you treat each other, and what to expect from one another. You can then create a board or collage displaying these values proudly. If children are involved in this process, they feel more connected and responsible for meeting these expectations.

128. Start practicing setting a daily affirmation. Each morning before you and your child go to school/work, make up an affirmation together for the day. Affirmations help us set positive intentions and what we want from our day. Your daily affirmations with your child might reflect something that didn't go well the day before, or something they would like to see happen that day. "Today I will be patient and take my time. I don't need to rush."

129. Find them stories to read that demonstrate kindness, giving, and compassion. You can find a great range of picture books right up to young adult novels that meet this brief. If you have a teenager, you can also read the book and spend some time thinking about interesting questions to pose to them to get them reflecting on the topic and thinking about kindness.

130. Create a gratitude grab bag. Have a bowl, cup, or box (that you can decorate together as another fun activity) which you fill up with "compliment slips." Each note included in the box expresses gratitude for something the person has done—for example, "I'm so grateful you helped me with my homework"—or just a general note of appreciation: "I'm so glad you are my son/daughter." When they are feeling a bit flat, sad, or just need a pick-me-up, they can grab a note from their grab bag box. This way they will experience what it is like to be on the receiving end of kindness (which builds empathy), but also learn to demonstrate their appreciation of others. You can even extend the idea so that everyone in the family has their own grab bag box.

131. Find books that explore and highlight groups of people who belong to a different "group" than your child; this could include different cultures, religions, etc. The message is not to find or highlight those differences, but rather to build their empathy and understanding of what the world is like and how it is experienced by different groups of people. You can find books on these topics from picture books right up to young adult novels.

132. *Watch age-appropriate TV shows with them and play a game. See how many emotions they can correctly identify for the characters in the show. Ask them how they know the answer to this. And why do they think the character is experiencing a particular feeling?*

133. You want to ensure that your child does not feel shamed by making mistakes. You can do this by encouraging them to reach out and ask for help, rather than taking action that might not be the best option. Sometimes asking for help is seen as a sign of weakness, but you want them to learn that it is not weak, but strong. So, if they do make a mistake, ask them what they needed to learn or consider so the mistake doesn't happen again and encourage them to see who could help them make decisions before they do make a mistake. For example, instead of just writing any answer down on their homework because they are worried about the consequences of not finishing it, get them to come to you to ask if you know the answers or how to help them. Or they could approach their teacher before school to explain why they didn't do it and ask for some extra help understanding the question.

134. Play the Empathy Matching Game. Write down a few scenarios as well as some corresponding feeling words and get your child to match the two. An example of a scenario might be: One kid in the playground is hogging the swing and will not let anyone else play on it. You could then get them to think about how the other children in the playground might be feeling. Support them to match an emotion (anger, frustration, sadness, surprise) to this scenario and encourage them that there is no right or wrong answer. Essentially, you want them thinking about how other people might be feeling; this is empathy and is an essential component of kindness.

135. Spend time with your family and take them on a simple outing to a park, river, forest, etc. Make sure you pack a camera and take some photos to record your trip and the things you see. When you get home, sit down and look at them together and get each person to pick their favorite photo and talk about why they like it so much. This will get your child reflecting and showing appreciation and gratitude for something simple.

136. TV time takes away from spending time together. It reduces your child's capacity to interact with others. Spending time with different people and in different settings helps them learn problem solving and negotiation skills and increases their ability to communicate. These are all essential skills required to demonstrate kindness.

137. If you can't limit TV time (hey, I'm a realistic and practical mom, too, I get it!), then enhance their experience by getting them to reflect on what they are watching. What do they like or dislike about the show? What feelings does the show or characters bring up for them? Are there any moral lessons that they can take away? Can they identify any of the feelings of the characters on the show?

138. Talk to your child about boundaries. What is a boundary? What are their boundaries? And why? It's important that they know their own limits and are empowered to keep themselves

safe, but also help them understand that others have boundaries they need to respect.

139. Encourage them to speak up and tell you or a teacher if they see bullying (in person or online). Even if they are not the person being the bully, or being bullied, you don't want your child to accept these kinds of behaviors and just stand by.

140. Write thank-you notes, with your child's help, to appreciate gifts they have been given. Discuss why it is important to show our appreciation.

CHAPTER 5

MANAGING DESTRUCTIVE FEELINGS

An element of developing kindness is also centered around a child's ability to regulate their emotions (when faced with a challenge) and delaying their own gratification to meet the needs of others (including individuals and groups). If a child cannot learn to do this, then making a choice to engage in kind acts is very challenging. One example that comes to mind is a ten-year-old boy I worked with whose parents reported concerns about his friendships because he often came home in trouble for fighting during school. When we explored this in counseling, I eventually uncovered that he often dominated play with his friends and chose all the games or activities they played at recess. He seemed unwilling to take turns and share the choice of games; he was not able to put his own needs and wants aside for the needs of others, which seriously impacted the quality of his friendships. In part, this was because he wasn't able to adequately assess the emotional state of his peers, and because he couldn't understand what they were feeling, he found it hard to modify his behavior in socially appropriate ways. As our sessions progressed, we worked on the basics of identifying different types of emotions and exploring his understanding of where different emotions might come from, as well as his capacity to apply this understanding to other people (being empathetic). This sounds a bit complex, but essentially, when he was able to recognize different emotions in other people, it helped him make decisions that were kind, because he empathized and understood how his actions were affecting people. He also learned some strategies to regulate his feelings in more productive and healthy ways. At the end of our time together, both he and his parents reported that his relationships had improved in number and quality and he was not getting in so many arguments with peers.

EMOTIONAL INTELLIGENCE

Social and emotional skills are essential for our children. Our society seems to be placing more focus on academic achievement and less on the social and emotional needs that help our children navigate the world. What use is mental arithmetic when calculating how to split a receipt at dinner if you don't have any friends to share the dinner with? Throughout my years working in play therapy with children, I have had dozens of calls from educators who asked what magic I was working in the sessions with our mutual client/student. They had noticed a remarkable turnaround in the child's educational achievement as well as less disruption or challenging behaviors in the classroom. Although it might have seemed like "magic" and the student was far more socially appropriate in the classroom, my focus in counseling and play therapy has never been to make children "compliant" or be able to follow rules. For me, the key to happy and mentally healthy children is all about developing their emotional intelligence.

So How Does Emotional Intelligence Make People Kind?

As with other strategies I have already talked about, teaching emotional intelligence starts at home. As soon as children can vocalize, they are capable of communicating about their feelings. Because emotions are pretty much automatic and are innate, we can easily forget to focus on teaching children about feelings; how to recognize them, name them, and respond to them appropriately. However, in my opinion, parents should place just as much emphasis on teaching their children about feelings as they do on teaching them about counting, naming colors, and spelling. Although these are obviously essential skills that children need to learn in our society, our emotional intelligence is just as important (if not more so!). We have emotions for a reason—just like everything else in our body, they serve a purpose. Humans have a biological need to connect and form relationships; this is what makes us thrive as a species. Research does show that people who feel lonely or don't have opportunities to experience close and mutually beneficial

> **Key Definition**
>
> Emotional intelligence: the ability of a person to recognize emotions and manage them; this includes their own emotions as well as other peoples.

relationships can experience higher levels of stress, health issues, lowered immunity, sleep disturbance, and generally lower well-being.[1, 2] Children who have a higher level of emotional intelligence are more likely to have successful relationships, and this is associated with a higher quality of life.

So where does kindness come into this? Essentially, having a higher emotional intelligence allows people to understand how another person might feel, which allows them to respond or engage with the person and meet their emotional needs. This "response" to someone else's needs is being kind. So, an example of how this might play out: it's the first day of school and two children are in the schoolyard. One notices the other sitting alone with tears in their eyes. They sit next to the other child and say, "Are you lonely? You look sad. Would you like to come and play?" The other child is likely to feel comforted and less distressed after having their feelings acknowledged in this way. This ability to recognize and respond to other people's emotions (emotional intelligence) in a compassionate way (kindness) is what helps build relationships, which we humans crave. So, by improving your child's emotional intelligence, it helps develop their ability to be kind, as they will be able to respond compassionately and empathically to those around them.

Emotional intelligence is also crucial to developing kindness, but in a very different way than I described above. The two most common issues I have seen in counseling over the years (for both adults and children) is when people deny their feelings (or have difficulty identifying them), and the second is when they respond to their feelings in inappropriate ways. Both can result in frustration, fear, not getting their needs met, feeling overwhelmed or stressed, and sometimes adopting unhealthy ways of distracting themselves from the pain of those feelings. These all make it difficult to be kind, as the person's focus is on themselves and their own needs (which, of course, are important) but can hinder them from considering others.

As a parent, if you don't have a particularly healthy way of dealing with your feelings, it might feel challenging at times to show your child how to manage their emotions in a healthy and adaptive way. This isn't a judgment on you as a parent or a person, and it's perfectly okay if you feel like this describes you (or sometimes describes you). However, it is important to acknowledge if you struggle with this, because your child watches the way that you respond to challenges and situations in your life for guidance as to how they should react. Fortunately, we can retrain ourselves and increase our emotional intelligence at any age, and I have some really clear activities that you can do with your child to really explore and expand their understanding of their emotions. There are many techniques that I will mention in the next chapter, but there are five key things that make up emotional intelligence and underpin the activities I have outlined. I like to use the RULER acronym.[3]

- **R**—recognizing emotions in ourselves and others
- **U**—understanding the cause and impact of emotions
- **L**—labeling emotions correctly
- **E**—expressing emotions in healthy and appropriate ways
- **R**—regulating emotions

Diagnosing Emotions

An important element of empathy is being able to identify facial emotional expressions in others. To learn this skill, your child might need to put on their detective hat! First, it is important to teach them the key or universal emotions: anger, sadness, fear, joy, surprise, disgust, and contempt. The reason these emotions are "universal" is that, regardless of a person's background, these are emotions that all nations and cultures identify in the same way, i.e. everyone knows a certain facial expressions mean anger and it is the same around the world.[4] Second, it is important to teach them how to identify each different feeling, and below I have created an outline of what each emotion looks like as a facial expression.

Anger
- Eyebrows are pulled down
- Lower eyelids are pulled up
- Edge/side of the lips are curled in
- Lips may be pursed

Disgust
- Eyebrows are pulled down
- Nose is wrinkled
- Lips are loose and upper lip is pulled up

Fear
- Eyebrows are pulled up and closer together
- Eyelids are raised
- The mouth is stretched wide

Joy
- Skin around the eyes is tight, creating crow's-feet or crinkles around the eyes
- Cheeks are raised
- The corners of the lips are raised toward the cheeks

Sadness
- The inner eyebrows are tight and raised
- Eyelids are loose
- Mouth is loose and dropped slightly at the edges

Contempt
- Eyes don't move/change
- Lip is lifted up on one side only (sneer)

Surprise
- Entire length of the eyebrow is tightened and lifted
- Eyelids are pulled up
- Mouth is open (but not tight)

Encouraging this "detective" skill in your child will help them better navigate social situations and increase their ability to correctly identify the emotional needs of others. This is especially important because we know that sometimes a person's words don't always match their true feelings. For example, your child's friend might be quite upset, but when asked how they are doing, they reply "I'm fine!" although they are, in fact, not fine at all. Most of the time, a person's nonverbal cues will give away their true feelings. Going back to the previous example, if your child's friend said,

"I'm fine!" in a soft and wavering voice, while bowing their head down, or screamed "I'm fine!" while stamping their foot . . . it's a pretty good indication that their verbal and nonverbal messages are not congruent. If your child is skilled at identifying nonverbal cues for different emotions, it allows them to demonstrate kindness because they are able to understand how others are truly feeling and respond to them in a way congruent to their feelings, not just reacting to what they are saying out loud.

EXPRESSING EMOTIONS IN A HEALTHY WAY

Not only do we need to teach our children how to identify their own and others' emotions, but we also need to equip them with the skills to regulate their feelings in healthy and adaptive ways. Part of this is about acknowledging, understanding, and accepting their emotions as normal and important functions of the body and mind. Sometimes, because an emotion doesn't feel good, we are tempted to avoid or rid ourselves of the feeling, and this can start in childhood. Have you ever said to your child "Don't cry!" or "Cheer up, it's okay!"? If you have, you aren't alone. When our children hurt, we really want to take away their pain, and this can inadvertently lead to us rushing them through their feeling or trying to distract them from it. Not because we are mean, but because we want to spare our children from being in pain. However, without intending to, these kinds of statements de-emphasize the feelings or experiences of children; they can also teach them that feelings are shameful or even something to be avoided. Avoidance in particular can actually make a feeling seem even more out of control or that their feelings are something to be frightened of.

Some of the biggest fears my clients have reported is that they worry they will never experience any other emotion again, or that they will be overwhelmed by the magnitude of the feeling. However, rather than being scared of big emotions, it can be helpful to build your child's understanding that every emotion serves some kind of purpose, either by protecting us (physically, or emotionally) or giving us some useful information about ourselves, the environment, or others around us. It might feel counterintuitive or even distressing for you, but allow your children to sit with their distress. It also might not be pleasant, but it teaches them that feelings are just that! They are only feelings, and they won't last forever. It also helps to improve their confidence and belief that they can manage their feelings and that they won't be overwhelmed by them. By sitting with their feelings and not rushing them to feel "better," you are also showing them that you value their emotional experiences, e.g., "It is okay to be sad because you are really disappointed you didn't win," or "I can see you are angry that you aren't being listened to."

This brings me to another important point: feelings themselves are okay, but we do need to give our children guidance for expressing them in healthy ways. Sometimes when children push down their feelings or don't have the right guidance, they may learn to express their feelings in negative and destructive ways, and often their emotions are turned outward toward other people; for example, feeling angry and shouting at someone, or feeling sad and blocking other people out. Difficulty regulating their emotions in healthy and adaptive ways can negatively influence other people, so this is a key concept in teaching your child to be kind.

DELAYING GRATIFICATION

Being able to delay gratification is an important skill, and it is very reliant on your child being able to regulate their emotions. Delaying gratification is all about being able to put off (or delay) an immediate "want" for a later time, knowing that if they wait, there will be a better opportunity or an improved outcome at some point in the future. The "Marshmallow Test" was part of a study into the ability of children to delay gratification.[5, 6] Children were presented with a plate that had one marshmallow on it (or another type of sweet treat) and were told that the researcher had to leave the room for a few minutes. If the child didn't eat the marshmallow while the researcher was out of the room, the child would be rewarded with two marshmallows to eat. However, if they couldn't wait, they were told to ring a bell and the researcher would come back and the child could eat the marshmallow on the plate but wouldn't get a second one. This was a really fascinating look into willpower, which is what it takes to delay that instant desire to eat the marshmallow to get a better outcome of two marshmallows instead. If you have a moment of spare time, get on the Internet and look up some videos of this test being conducted. Watching the different ways children cope with this challenge, the strategies they use to delay gratification or inventive ways they try to get around the rules of not eating the marshmallow, are pretty inventive and a little amusing.

So why is the ability to delay gratification so important, and what does it have to do with kindness? Delaying an immediate need for a later goal is incredibly important to the overall success and well-being of your child in later life. Who knew marshmallows could predict this kind of stuff?! This is because children who can delay their initial desire for that one marshmallow in order to be given two have the skills required to stay motivated for some bigger goal.

- This can directly translate to better financial security, because they can save money for a bigger or more important purchase rather than frittering away their money on small or impulsive purchases.
- They are also more likely to experience occupational prestige. Instead of taking a moderately paid job (instant money), they have the motivation to complete additional studies/ courses/training or stay in a job for later promotional opportunities to get a better job in the long term (limited money to begin with, but with a greater windfall in the future).
- Being able to delay gratification is also associated with positive mental health, including increased self-worth, as it uses a similar skill set required for adaptive emotional coping and resilience.
- Children who undertook the original "Marshmallow Test" were contacted as teenagers and they were found to have a higher level of social competence, which equates to more friends and better-quality relationships. The ability to delay gratification also helps children practice kindness. It gives them the skills to put off their own needs for the greater good of the group or in support of someone else's needs or wants. An ability to recognize and adapt behavior to help and support someone else is likely to be part of the reason why those who can delay gratification experience higher-quality relationships.

SELF-REGULATION

Being able to manage feelings and behaviors (that occur in response to those feelings) is called self-regulation. This skill is important in developing kindness, because if emotions aren't expressed in appropriate ways, they can sometimes hurt, distress, or upset other people around us, which might be unintentional, but still not particularly kind. For example, we all feel angry at some point, but we learn that there are appropriate times/places and ways of expressing our emotions. It is appropriate to tell someone you feel angry, or go for a run to get rid of some of the emotional energy that comes with anger, but it isn't really appropriate to scream in the face of someone who has annoyed you. Anger itself is actually a normal and necessary emotion, but when we feel angry sometimes, we want to lash out, or physically express our outrage, or possibly want other people to hurt as much as we do.

Children go through very normal phases of testing boundaries and also have to explicitly learn how to manage their feelings in appropriate ways. Most toddlers or young children will go through stages of hitting, screaming, biting, pinching, etc. It is often (but not always) because they are trying to express their emotions, namely frustration. It takes the gentle guidance of their parents (that's you!) to help them understand what they are feeling (think back to the RULER method) and give them the tools to express their emotions in more adaptive and socially appropriate ways.

Emotional regulation starts very early, from birth, in fact. Infants are exposed to many new things like sights, smells, and other sensations that can be confusing and frightening. Crying and showing their distress is the only way they can communicate. From birth to around eighteen months of age, your job (during this stage of their life) is to comfort them. This is also the beginning stage of their learning about emotional regulation. When you pick up your child and cuddle them, hold them close, kiss them, whisper to them, etc., it brings their distress back down to tolerable levels. Although it seems like such a natural thing to comfort a crying infant, what you are teaching them is that distress doesn't last forever, and they are able to be comfortable and safe again. They also learn that if they express their needs, others will recognize and help them meet their needs; infants learn that a gurgle might make you smile, a cry will bring help (or food), and a grimace might bring comfort. In these moments, your child is laying down connections in their brain that strengthen the relationships between their feelings, their needs, and how they can communicate them.

The next stage of emotional regulation occurs during infancy and toddlerhood around the time that they are starting to pick up and use language. In the first stage, your infant is reliant on you to interpret and help them modulate their feelings, but this next stage is all about your child learning to express themselves and communicate their inner (emotional) experiences. As your child learns to speak, they will begin to use language in a more organized and coherent way. This stage of emotional regulation is all about giving your child the right words, through repetition and reflection, to be able to identify their feelings. When your child becomes consciously aware of different emotions, it gives them the skill to attach a particular feeling to an event, and then they can act accordingly and take the next step of regulating their emotions. It sounds a bit fancy, but when you break it down, you essentially want to help your child make sense of their chaos. This is typically why we see tantrums during toddlerhood. Our children are going through a big stage of emotional growth and development, they have big feelings, but if they don't know how to name them or understand where they came from, or indeed what to do with them, they can become quickly overwhelmed. So even the simple act of teaching your child different words for different feelings is giving them a sense of order and control, which can increase their confidence that they can manage those big, overwhelming sensations associated with emotions.

Each emotional stage of development builds on the skills perfected in the previous stage. By the time your toddler reaches preschool, they should have enough language and knowledge to distinguish between a wide range of feelings. They use this skill to expand their self-regulation abilities and go from being able to just communicate their emotions and needs to others to also developing self-talk, or that internal system that guides them (review the previous chapter on the importance of a positive inner voice). During the early schooling years right through to early adulthood, children are also laying down more pathways in the brain in the prefrontal cortex; this is the part of the brain that allows us to use logic and reasoning. Your child will begin to talk about their feelings, manage complex social situations, and avoid emotional outbursts because they have not only learned the skills to communicate their emotions, but they can also make connections between their emotions and what they need to do to meet their own emotional needs.

I worked with a six-year-old boy who was referred for play therapy sessions to address "anger issues." To start, I don't really like this term *anger issues*; there is a lot of confusion between anger and aggression. *Anger* is the emotion, it is perfectly normal, adaptive, and healthy, but *aggression*, on the other hand, is a way that some people choose to express their anger. Anyway, this young boy had a lot of trouble regulating feelings of anger; he would have verbal outbursts and get physical, lashing out at others and himself when he was feeling angry. The school was concerned because he was hurting other children and was quite aggressive toward teaching staff, as well. We had to start right back at the early stages of emotional regulation and worked on developing his vocabulary of emotional words (I have included some of the activities we did in the next chapter). I spent a lot of time reflecting emotion while he was playing: "It seems like you are really mad you didn't win that game" and "I can tell you are frustrated that the tower you are building fell over." These seem like simple enough reflections, but they gave him the opportunity to make sense of his internal, chaotic feelings. Once he could differentiate between different feelings and could put a name to them, it was easier to come up with strategies to help him regulate his emotions. So, we worked on noticing the early stages of his emotions—frustrated versus enraged so that he could preempt his aggressive outbursts and put in place some calming strategies like relaxation breathing, exerting some of his energy in healthy, physical ways (like doing star jumps or jumping jacks, kicking a ball outside, and playing on his drum kit), and also moving away from triggering situations (where safe and appropriate). Once he was able to practice these skills, both he and his parents reported less angry outbursts at school. His teachers reported he was much kinder toward his peers, respectful of their personal boundaries, more able to engage in social interactions without becoming aggressive, and that he was making friends.

It may not feel like a direct link, but teaching your child all about their emotions and how to manage them will allow them to demonstrate kindness to their peers. It allows children to use the knowledge they have of their own emotions and apply it to other people, which is a key skill/ability associated with empathy. The next chapter has some really clear tips that will help you teach your child about different feelings as well as some targeted strategies for regulating different emotions.

REFLECTION EXERCISES—MANAGING DESTRUCTIVE FEELINGS

1. What is your go-to emotion when things don't go your way or life stressors arise?

2. What are your primary coping strategies for different emotions? Are they behaviors you want your child to replicate?

3. Which emotion are you most fearful of or try to avoid the most often? Why?

CHAPTER 6
TIPS FOR MANAGING DESTRUCTIVE FEELINGS

141. Teach them how to STOP when they feel over-whelmed. This one is also a great tip for parents. Unless there is a safety issue that needs immediate attention, there is nothing else that needs an instanta-neous response.
     - "S" stands for Stop. Get them to physically stand still. This helps ground them and delays or even stops them from rushing into something or reacting without thinking.
     - "T" stands for Take a deep breath. A deep, relaxing breath (or five) helps reset the nervous

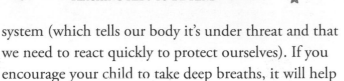

system (which tells our body it's under threat and that we need to react quickly to protect ourselves). If you encourage your child to take deep breaths, it will help them relax and allow the rational/logical part of their brain kick back in to gear.

- "O" stands for Observe. Get them to observe the feelings in their body and acknowledge them (angry, sad, frightened, etc.). By observing their bodies and feelings, they will usually be able to figure out what emotion they are having and possibly why they are having it. This can reduce the intensity or power of the emotions; therefore, your child is less likely to react in a heightened way. Observing also gives them precious space to make a conscious decision rather than reacting.

- "P" stands for Proceed, or carry on. Once they have had a chance to take stock of a situation and given themselves a little breather, it's easier to make kinder and more socially appropriate choices in the face of stress. So, this step is about taking action after they have taken a breath and acknowledged how they feel.

142. *Play an emotions bingo game. Everyone gets a different bingo card with different emotions. Watch a movie as a family and cross off different emotions on your card until someone gets "bingo!"*

143. Mindful Walking, part 1. Mindfulness activities are all about clearing the mind of lots of chatter (or possibly negative thoughts) and focusing on the present moment. Take a walk

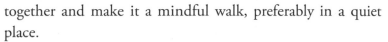
together and make it a mindful walk, preferably in a quiet place.

144. Mindful Walking, part 2. Count your steps. Count up to ten (or perhaps twenty, but not too many more or you may become distracted) and then start again. Focus only on your counting and stepping.

145. Mindful Walking, part 3. Press your hands gently to your belly (just above your belly button) and notice the movements of your hands as you breathe while you are walking. Can you notice any change as you walk faster or slower (and your breathing changes)?

146. Mindful Walking, part 4. Walking for the senses. While you are walking, take turns focusing on some different senses (touch, smell, sound, sight) and set an alarm for two minutes. See how much information you gather about each sense in the time frame. For example, stop in a clearing and listen for 2 minutes. What can you hear? How many different noises? As you listen, are the noises changing or evolving?

147. Mindful Walking, part 5. Go for a short walk and pay attention to the weight of your step as you press your foot into the ground. Notice how the weight changes from the heel of your foot to the ball of your foot and then your toes. Focus on the sensation of your foot as you stand on different surfaces and ask yourself: is the surface firm? Or does it have some give? Is it even? Or uneven? Is it flat or on an incline? And for added benefits, try this mindful walk barefoot if it's safe to do so.

148. Introduce a feelings thermometer to help your child recognize and process their feelings. Draw a thermometer with temperatures starting at 0, right up to 100 (from the bottom to the top of the thermometer). Explore with your child that

0 means calm, or no strong feelings, and 100 (the top of the thermometer) means the biggest or most intense feeling they can imagine. First, ask them what emotions they are experiencing, then give them a sticker to adhere to the picture, or get them to point to indicate how intense their feeling is. Second, ask them what they think would help bring their emotion to a level they would be happy with. Please note that if the feelings are intense (over 70–80), they might need some help regulating themselves down.

149. Create a set of cards with emotion pictures on one side. You could either get your child to draw them, or find some online and print them out. On the opposite side of the card, you would then encourage your child to draw or write a strategy/item/idea/activity that will help them balance out or counteract that particular feeling. You could make as many cards as you need to match the number of ideas they have about balancing different feelings. One example might be a picture of a sad face on one side of the card and a drawing of some music notes, depicting that listening to a specific piece of music might help your child tolerate feelings of sadness.

150. Introduce the "Feelings in My Body Game." Draw an outline of a human body and give your child a variety of different colored pens/pencils/crayons. Ask them to match colors to the different feelings that they experience in their body (prompts might be "what color should anger be?" and "what about scared?"). Then get them to color in where they feel different feelings in their body (e.g., they might color blue/sadness around the eyes, or throat, anger/red in their fists or jaw). It doesn't matter where they color, or what colors they

choose to represent each moment, the point is getting them to reflect on their own internal experiences.

151. Do an Internet search and find some images of faces (kids and adults) with different emotional expressions, like sad, angry, happy, surprised, etc. Create some flash cards with images on the front and the emotion written on the back. Ask them questions about what emotion they think is being displayed and why they think the person is having that particular feeling. This activity will build empathy but also self-awareness. Kids are generally focused on themselves and their own experiences (so what they have witnessed, or what they have personally experienced), and they will draw on this knowledge to answer your questions.

152. *There are seven key emotions universally recognized and displayed; this means that regardless of culture, upbringing etc., these emotions look and are interpreted the same way. Teach your child to name and identify these key emotions: anger, fear, disgust, contempt, joy, sadness, and surprise.*

153. Print pictures of people displaying the seven key emotions (anger, fear, disgust, contempt, joy, sadness, and surprise). It is preferable if they are pictures of real people rather than cartoons, but you could use either. Use the "Diagnostic Tool" in the previous chapter (page 78) about emotional regulation to point at different parts of the face (e.g., raised eyebrows, mouth that is turned down) as a tool to help your child learn about how to identify the different emotions you have

printed out. It can be a bit of a guessing game and a fun activity for kids who enjoy playing detective.

154. If you have a much younger child or toddler, they can still learn to differentiate emotions; however, you might start with a simplified list to teach them. For example, you can focus on three key feelings: mad, sad, and glad, or for younger children, you might introduce the concept of emotions by asking they are experiencing a good or bad feeling.

155. Emotional Traffic Light, part 1. Create an emotional traffic light system to use to explore anger. You or your child can draw a rectangle with three circles inside (to represent a traffic light). Color the lights in the appropriate order: green, amber/orange, and red. These colors represent emotional distress as it progresses; green means your child is calm and good to go. Amber means your child is starting to feel frustrated and that they need to slow down and think about some strategies to regulate their feelings. And red means your child has become overwhelmed, angry, and they need to stop. Usually a parent or other adult needs to help them regulate their feelings by the time they reach the red light! Next to the amber and red lights, come up with a list of strategies to help bring their distress down or to self soothe so that they can begin to move back into the green light. Every child will be different, so the list of things that work will be different for everyone. In the section next to the amber light, remember that these are activities the child can do themselves, and the tips for the red light are strategies you can help them with to de-escalate.

156. Emotional Traffic Light, part 2. "Orange" Emotional Traffic Light strategies. Encourage your child to work with you to create a list of activities or actions that can help them slow

down (and you can explain the traffic light system to them. Orange/amber = slow). Every child will have different preferences, but some ideas might be: move away from the situation or trigger (if safe to do so), count to ten, do five relaxation breaths, go for a walk, read a book, do a drawing, etc. Because the emotion hasn't built up to intolerable levels, these are activities that can distract them or are positive (to counteract the distressing emotion). These are generally activities that they can do independently.

157. Emotional Traffic Light, part 3. "Red" Emotional Traffic Light strategies. By the time your child reaches the danger zone, they will most likely need your help to regulate themselves back down. Even though they might need your assistance at this stage, continue to involve them in helping identify the strategies that are best going to work to regulate their distress. Do this work beforehand or at a time they are in the green; they will find it challenging to be part of a logical conversation and planning by the time they reach the red light. They may already feel out of control by the time they get to this stage, so you don't want to accidentally disempower them further by doing things without their permission or they haven't agreed to. Some strategies might include: star jumps or jumping jacks, kick a ball (at the park or somewhere safe), five relaxation breaths, scream into a pillow, squish some dough in their hands, etc. The strategies at this stage might need to be more physical to help them use some of the emotional energy associated with anger.

158. Emotional Traffic Light, part 4. Alternative ways to use the Emotional Traffic Light system, part 1. You could also draw pictures next to each traffic light color that remind your child

what each traffic light color feels like and help them record their response (drawing or writing). For example, orange might feel tightness in their jaw or fists, feeling sick in their tummy, getting warm (temperature, etc.). Red might feel like clenching teeth, sweating, shaking, feeling hot, flushed face, etc.

159. Emotional Traffic Light, part 5. Alternative ways to use the Emotional Traffic Light system, part 2. Depending on the emotional needs of your child, and as they become increasingly aware of their feelings, you might create a number of different Traffic Light systems; one for anger, one for sadness, one for when they are scared.

160. *When you decide to have any discussions or negotiations about consequences, your child's behavior, or plans to help them regulate their emotions, do it when they are calm. They may find it very challenging to negotiate or to be be rational or reasonable when they are already distressed/ overwhelmed/upset.*

161. Grow a plant together. Your child will need to take very good care of it in order for it to grow. This will teach them patience and delayed gratification and will encourage them to be nurturing. Generally, edible plants or very vibrant/showy flowers work well, as there is some kind of tangible reward for your child's patience.

162. Do a complex puzzle (complexity in this case will be age dependent). Set it up on a table or stable surface somewhere so you can come back to it periodically. It takes time and persistence to find all of the pieces and fit them together, so a puzzle is an ideal way to teach delayed gratification. They can only see the finished piece (and that sense of accomplishment) if they complete the entire puzzle.

163. Create a game of "Snap" using printed images of paired emotions glued onto the back of playing cards. For younger children, you could use the same image replicated twice or four times to create easier opportunities to "snap" a matching pair of cards. For older kids, you could use the same emotion, like anger, but with two pictures of different people expressing anger to make the game more challenging.

164. Create a game of emotional memory to play with your child. Create pairs of emotions by printing images of people expressing emotions and sticking them to the back of playing cards. Lay down the cards with the emotional faces and try to recall where all of the matching pairs are. For younger children, only lay out a few pairs with exact matching images. Increase the challenge for older children and print out different images that express the same emotions and have more cards (i.e., more possible emotions) to try and locate.

165. Create a list of emotional words that range in intensity. For example, sad can range from "flat" at the lower end of intensity right up to "distraught" or "grief" at the higher end of the intensity spectrum. Ask your child to group the emotional words under a headings of Sad, Angry, Happy/Joy, Surprised, Scared, and Disgusted and then get them to put the words in order of intensity (low to high). There is no real right or wrong answer, but if your child puts something that doesn't seem to fit, ask them what they think the word means and

why they put it in a particular order. When your child has lots of words to describe their feelings, they will become confident in understanding and being able to manage those feelings. Please review the resources at the end of this book if you would like some inspiration for a feelings list.

166. Play the "Feelings in my Heart" game. Print out or draw a picture of a love heart. Ask your child to create a pie chart, or color-code the heart to show how much their heart is full of a particular feeling. Get them to think about the color they are matching to each emotion. You can ask heaps of follow-up questions to really explore their emotions. Why did they choose a specific color to match an emotion? Why is their heart really full of a particular emotion? What do they wish their heart was full of instead, and why? What could they do to try and make the different proportions/percentages change to be closer to what they want?

167. *Slow down! We often cram as many activities as we can into our children's schedules thinking that it will help them become well-rounded individuals. But music lessons on Monday, karate on Tuesday, drama club on Wednesdays, etc. is too much. Children need time and space and to play spontaneously (this type of play helps them process their thoughts and reactions to events in their environment). So, try not to have rigid plans every day of the week. It allows your child space to play and work through any emotional or stressful events.*

168. Play the "Thoughts in my Head" game. Draw or print out a picture of a brain (just an outline is fine . . . you don't want too much detail, since they will be drawing/coloring inside the image of the brain). Get your child to write down or draw what kinds of thoughts they have had today. This activity, especially when paired with the "Feelings in my Heart" game, is a really vital way of teaching children the difference between thoughts and feelings. You can then also follow up with questions about their thoughts, reflecting and acknowledging their thoughts. You could even go further and ask them how particular thoughts make them feel.

169. Children need to be able to delay gratification. It is a skill that allows them to be kind, as they sometimes need to be able to delay their own wants/needs for the benefit of other people. The Internet has a lot to answer for in regard to diminished ability to delay gratification. This is because the instant accessibility of the Internet feeds into lack of "waiting" or the need to have immediate results/outcomes—everything is accessible at the click of a button; information, social connection, shopping, etc. If your child asks you a question, don't turn to the Internet immediately. Take them to the library or pull out some old reference books to research the answer. This teaches them the art of persistence and needing to maintain motivation to meet a goal.

170. Teaching them to self-soothe, part 1. Your child needs to learn different ways to settle themselves, especially if they are feeling distressed. If they do not learn this skill, they may become destructive, frustrated, or turn to unhealthy ways of releasing their emotions. It is important to think about how to counteract a particular emotion, rather than denying or getting rid

of it. First, help your child figure out what emotion they are experiencing. You could show them pictures (see other tips for examples) of different emotions to try and figure it out.

171. Teaching them to self-soothe, part 2. Work on a poster together or a brainstorming activity where you work on listing all the different activities your child can do to help themselves feel better. It works best if you find different strategies for particular emotions (as their needs will change dependent on the emotion). You could draw pictures or cut out pictures from magazines or print them out from the Internet to make a collage of different self-soothing activities. Ensure that the activities are appropriate, so they might need some guidance. The poster or brainstorm you create will serve as a prompt; this is important, because in the moment of distress, it can be hard to be rational/logical and recall these strategies.

172. Teaching them to self-soothe, part 3. This is an expansion of the previous tip. Some ideas for particular emotions might include:

- Anger—usually activities that allow them to get rid of excess energy work the best, just make sure the activities aren't violent or aggressive. Examples might include star jumps/jumping jacks, kicking a ball at the park, squeezing something like playdough, or kneading bread. They can sing really (really) loudly, jump on the trampoline, or run very fast.
- Sadness—play some upbeat dancing music, sit in the sunshine, read or tell a funny joke, look at pictures of fun times (birthday/holidays, etc)
- Fear—take some deep breaths, snuggle under a blanket, have a cuddle, grab their comfort item or favorite toy.

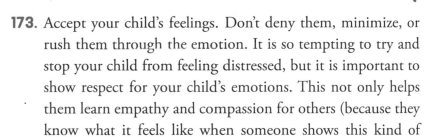

173. Accept your child's feelings. Don't deny them, minimize, or rush them through the emotion. It is so tempting to try and stop your child from feeling distressed, but it is important to show respect for your child's emotions. This not only helps them learn empathy and compassion for others (because they know what it feels like when someone shows this kind of respect), but it also teaches them that emotions are nothing to be afraid of.

174. Teaching delayed-gratification strategies, part 1—avoidance. Essentially, you want to teach your child that out of sight means out of mind. For younger children, they might need your assistance to remove an object from their line of sight so they can forget about it. Whereas with older children, it's about teaching them to distance themselves from temptation so that they can wait (or delay gratification) until the time is right (e.g., no sweets unless they have finished their dinner). You could say something to your child like, "It is so hard to wait, but if we put the sweets up high, then we can't see them, so we won't be tempted to eat one before dinner." Eventually, they will internalize these thoughts and become equipped to remove temptation themselves.

175. Teaching delayed-gratification strategies, part 2—positive distraction strategies. Encourage your child to participate in a new activity. For younger children, you can simply engage yourself in an exciting activity, or at least be very animated with whatever you choose to play with. They will be so interested in what you are doing that they will want to find out and will subsequently get distracted from their initial interest. For older children, you can ask them what activity might be the most helpful to help them to wait: "Waiting is so tough!

What do you think you could do to keep busy while you wait for (insert temptation)?"

176. Teaching delayed-gratification strategies, part 3—don't replace the temptation with something worse! Just be mindful that if you are supporting your child in learning techniques to help them delay gratification, then you don't want to replace one temptation with another ("Well you can't have a cookie before dinner, but you can have a packet of chips"), or encourage/ allow a negative or socially inappropriate ways of coping with the distress of waiting (e.g., tantrums, being oppositional or even hurting themselves in response to being overwhelmed).

177. Teaching delayed-gratification strategies, part 4—self-talk. Teach your child to self-verbalize to help them delay their initial wants for a later reward. For younger children, it can simply be narrating to them "It's okay, soon you will get _____." For older children, it can be about helping them identify a mantra or words that can help them maintain motivation while they wait. So, it could be emphasizing the reward or end goal, or it could be about having a phrase to repeat, such as "In five minutes, I will get _____."

178. Teaching delayed-gratification strategies, part 5—visualization. For visual temptations, it can be helpful to encourage your child to use their imagination to help them delay gratification. For example, a lovely piece of cake could be visualized as Styrofoam instead. It helps them to think about their goal in a different way or can help them disengage from how tempting something might be. And Styrofoam certainly isn't as appealing as a delicious slice of cake, so it will help them delay that intense feeling of wanting that cake "Now!"

179. Teaching delayed-gratification strategies, part 6—anticipation. Sometimes waiting can be exciting. You know that sense of anticipation that builds as you count down to a family holiday or some other event you have really been looking forward to? You can encourage this in your child by counting down or ticking off time in the buildup to an event. For little kids, it could be a timer or looking at a clock for a few minutes while they wait to go to the library, or for older kids, it could be a calendar where they cross off days in anticipation of their birthday coming up later in the month. You are teaching them that waiting isn't always a bad thing!

180. Teaching delayed-gratification strategies, part 7—patience. Some things just take time, and our children need to learn that sometimes we need to wait to get the best outcome. Think about cooking: Certain ingredients might taste nice separately, but they aren't as good as when they are all combined and cooked to make a delicious meal. So, help your child practice the art of patience by setting up activities and games that require persistence, prolonged motivation, and a reward associated with waiting. This might include cooking, doing a puzzle, folding origami, building with blocks like LEGOs or Duplo, and playing hide-and-seek.

181. Emotion poster. Another way to help your child learn how to identify emotions is to find some pictures of faces displaying different feelings. You can make this into a craft activity with your child, printing, cutting out, and pasting pictures of different emotions on a poster. Or you can find heaps of resources/websites where you can purchase these posters. Display this poster somewhere prominent so that your child can view it often and learn or reflect on the way faces move and change to display different feelings.

182. Play the "How Big are your Feelings?" game with your child if you can see that they are feeling sad, angry, worried, etc. (but this would easily work with positive feelings, too, especially if you are trying to teach gratitude and acceptance of all feelings). Grab a piece of paper and draw a circle. Give them a whole bunch of colored pens, pencils, or crayons and ask them to fill the circle to show how big their feelings are. Encourage them to imagine that they are the circle: how much room in their body does the feeling take up? Getting them to reflect on the "size" of their feelings will help them figure out and better understand their emotions. Being able to do this will also help them learn compassion and empathy.

183. Teach your child relaxation breathing, part 1. You can find an app or find a video on the Internet to demonstrate the technique to your child, but essentially, when teaching relaxation breathing, you want your child to breathe in through their nose for the count of five and breathe out through their mouth for the count of five. You want to keep this as slow and steady as possible, otherwise they might hyperventilate or become dizzy. To make it easy to remember, encourage them to count in for five, out for five, and do five relaxation breaths.

184. Teach your child relaxation breathing, part 2. Give your child a balloon and practice slow and steady "out breaths" by blowing into a balloon. If you don't have a balloon, get them to imagine that when they are breathing out, they are trying to fill a balloon.

185. Teach your child relaxation breathing, part 3. Get your child to imagine that on the "out breath," they are blowing out

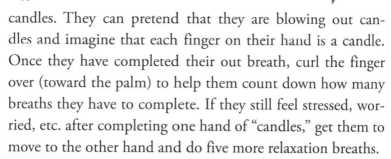

candles. They can pretend that they are blowing out candles and imagine that each finger on their hand is a candle. Once they have completed their out breath, curl the finger over (toward the palm) to help them count down how many breaths they have to complete. If they still feel stressed, worried, etc. after completing one hand of "candles," get them to move to the other hand and do five more relaxation breaths.

186. Encourage your child to express their feelings. Use a balloon analogy to help them understand why they need to talk about or deal with their emotions. Get a balloon and blow it up until it's nearly at bursting and tie it up. Ask them what would happen if you were playing with the balloon and it bounced against the wall or a toy? The answer is that it might burst, because it's full and very stretched. Tell them that this is like feelings; if our bodies and minds become too full, it doesn't take much for us to snap (or pop in the case of a balloon). Snapping doesn't feel very nice for us, and it can also accidentally hurt other people in the process. So, encourage them to let their feelings out by sharing or discussing with you, writing them down, or talking to a friend.

187. Create a self-regulation bottle, part 1. Keep an old (single-use) water bottle with a screw-on cap. Go through your craft box, if you have one, or see what art supplies you have lying around. Generally, you want to find different weighted items, so things like glitter, little pebbles or shiny gems, bouncy balls, beads, etc. Pop a few of these items in until they fill up around one-third of the bottle. There is no exact science, just make sure you get at least two tablespoons of glitter in. Then fill the bottle with water and seal the lid with glue; shutting it won't be enough, as you want to stop it from being opened again. You can use this bottle in a number of ways; for example, when your child is angry or distressed, get them to shake the bottle up as hard as they can. Then encourage them to try and sit still and keep their attention on the items in the bottle until the water has stopped swirling and all the items have settled to the bottom of the bottle again. This is essentially a technique similar to the STOP principles; sometimes just having a break and changing their focus can help them to begin to calm down.

188. Create a self-regulation bottle, part 2. You can also use the bottle as a metaphor to talk about feelings. You can explore with your child that sometimes feelings can get all mixed up like the items in the bottle, but if you give it enough time, everything does settle down again. You could also adapt it to say that sometimes we feel so rushed, our thoughts start to race, and sometimes we need to pause to let our thoughts slow down again.

189. Create a worry box or bag for your child. This could be something like a pencil case or a box with a tightly closing lid. The aim of the worry box/bag is that your child can write down things that are bothering or worrying them and feed them to the box, zip up the bag, or stick the lid back on. It gives children a chance to write down and acknowledge their worries without judgment. Expressing their fears also goes a long way toward processing them. You can even enjoy spending some time together decorating the box or bag.

190. Mindful eating. The purpose of this activity is to encourage your child to become aware of their actions, even the automatic ones like eating. Start with a wrapped sweet (it doesn't really matter what kind, but wrapped is better) or a raisin if

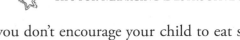

you don't encourage your child to eat sweets. Ask your child to hold the sweet in their hand and ask the following questions to get them really pay close attention:

- Is it warm? Cool?
- Heavy? Light?
- Soft? Hard?
- What shape is it?
- If you squeeze it in your palm (curl fingers around to completely hide the sweet in your hand), what does it feel like?
- Can you trace your finger around the edge of the sweet? What does it feel like?
- Okay, now unwrap the sweet. Can you smell anything?
- Pop the sweet on your tongue but don't chew/crunch/ lick it yet. Move the sweet to one side of your mouth and pop it in your cheek. Can you feel or taste anything different?
- Now, finally bite down on the sweet, just once. Is there much resistance? Is it hard or easy to bite down on? What does it sound like?
- All right, now you can chew and swallow the sweet when you are ready. Was that different than how you usually eat a sweet?
- Did it make the sweet taste any different?

191. Teach them patience and delayed gratification by baking a cake. This activity has the added bonus of spending time together, teamwork, and developing communication skills, as well. Find a recipe together and take turns following the instructions (or delegate particular tasks appropriate to their age-group/developmental level). Although there is an initial

reward and sense of pride in having followed the recipe, the reward of eating the cake is delayed. This helps your child truly appreciate the effort that has gone into their work and helps them see that some things take time and are worth waiting for.

192. Get your child to visualize that their feelings are visitors knocking on the door. Explain to them that we don't always know which "visitors" are going to visit or how long they will stay. But when a visitor does come over, we say hello and then watch them leave. You need to really stress the point that visitors don't live at their house, so they will always leave at some point. With this message, you are letting them know that they don't need to be afraid of their feelings, and despite worrying that they might never feel "better" again, that no feeling can last forever.

193. *Ask your child to imagine what their feelings look like. There is no right or wrong answer here—just encourage them to use their imagination! They might use colors or draw shapes or objects—it is entirely up to them. Visualizing helps them understand the impact of their emotions and also externalizes or allows them to see how their emotions might be affecting them, or what those feelings might represent.*

194. Ask them to draw what their feelings would look like if they were animals. You might need to give them some support to name a variety of different emotions.

195. Get your child to draw what they think their feelings would look like if they were people. Encourage them to think about

how big they are, what colors to use, features on their faces, clothes they are wearing, etc.

196. Allow your child to have space (both emotionally and physically) to find their own interests and activities. Sometimes we don't allow enough time for unstructured play, which is the type of play that allows children to consolidate learning and process things that have occurred throughout the day.

197. *Each day, set aside a certain amount of time for your child to choose their activities or games. Let them decide what they want to do; it will improve their sense of self-efficacy and self-esteem.*

198. Have a feelings chart on your wall, with pictures that represent key emotions. Encourage each family member to place themselves on this chart each morning before you leave the house and when you get home from work/school. Everyone has a laminated picture (with a Velcro dot or Blu Tack attached) that they can place on the board under their relevant feeling. Not only will this help your child recognize (and appreciate or take into consideration) the feelings of others, but also practice/develop an ability to recognize their own emotions. Being able to do this is linked with an increased ability to regulate (i.e., manage and contain) their feelings, which helps in the development of kindness.

199. *Brainstorm and come up with a project to do together, like building a garden bed. Not only will you be working together, but they will experience a sense of pride (an emotional reward) and heightened self-esteem when the project is completed.*

200. If your child invites a friend over to play, set up a teamwork activity. It will get them developing good communication skills and the ability to take turns, share, and cooperate—all of which are essential for kindness. It could be following a recipe and making a meal/baking, it could be following a treasure hunt you have set up for them. Anything that comes with a vague set of instructions to follow or rules and that relies on them working together for an outcome.

201. If your child is struggling with a particular skill, try and link them with a peer or even extended family member who is good at that skill. Encourage your child to ask this other person for help. Help-seeking teaches them positive communication, and also that it's okay if they aren't good at everything. They might also learn a new skill or get better at a certain activity, which will promote their confidence, self-belief, and resilience to "keep trying."

202. Limit screen time for your child. Research outlines that after even one hour of screen time, both children and teenagers show less curiosity, a reduced ability to regulate their emotions, lower self-control, and a diminished ability to complete tasks. These are all essential to being able to demonstrate kindness. Screen time also reduces the valuable time spent in the company of other people, where your child can practice face-to-face communication and strengthen their relationships.

CHAPTER 7
REWARDING KINDNESS

M ost parents use rewards in some way, usually to promote or have their children repeat a certain behavior. So, let's apply it to the topic of kindness. It seems simple enough: you see your child being kind so you reward them, right?! A candy bar in exchange for sharing their toys? Or a new toy when you hear about them being kind to the new kid in school? Unfortunately, it's a little more complicated than that. When talking about kindness, rewards can actually do the opposite of what you are intending.

A study conducted by Roth, Kanat-Maymon, and Bibi[7] on school bullying looked at the impact of students being given generous praise and strict sanctions/punishment to try and combat behaviors associated with bullying. The results showed that although, in the short term, students stopped bullying, there were no long-term changes to their behavior. This is because rewards increase an incentive to do something in the moment, but changes are only surface level. The study outlined that rewards also cease to have an impact in the long term; people become **habituated** to the reward, so it needs to keep increasing or changing in order to result in the same outcome. When talking about kindness (or any behavior, really), the same thing applies: if you reward kindness with material goods or praise, you might see an immediate change in your child. They may repeat the behavior that got them the initial reward, but this is because they want another reward, not because they have learned the value of kindness.

Okay, so if you are wondering why this chapter is titled "Rewards" when I am telling you that rewards are actually no good at promoting kindness, then please keep reading, I promise I am getting to the point. I also promise that while I am not encouraging rewards in a traditional

Key Definition

Habituated (habituate)—something that we get used to over time due to repetition/exposure.

sense, I absolutely have some tips to share that can help you shape the expectations you have for your child's behavior/actions/attitudes in relation to kindness and compassion.

So why don't rewards have any kind of long-term impact? Essentially, it is because material goods and even praise are external motivators; so, the reward is coming from something or somewhere outside themselves. We want to move our children from a place where they rely on **extrinsic motivators**, to a place where they rely on **intrinsic motivators** instead. This intrinsic motivation is what makes your child want to be kind again as the motivation come from their internal drive or desire to feel good about their choices which is what kindness is all about.

The reason rewards don't work for kindness (or any behavior, in all honesty) is that rewards are *self-serving*, but kindness is all about being *selfless*. Kindness is all about the ingrained, internalized desire to care for other people. When you use rewards, your child learns what they need to replicate (e.g., acts of kindness), but they aren't actually learning the value of being selfless and compassionate. You don't want your child to connect the reward to doing a kind deed, otherwise they are just learning that if they are outwardly kind, they will get something in return. This is materialism—not kindness—and is in fact the exact opposite of kindness, which is all about being selfless, altruistic, and empathetic. Now back to the topic (as promised): I'm not saying that you should never reward your child for demonstrating kindness, but I would recommend that you are aware of the following pitfalls and also consider the following alternatives that won't undo the hard work you are doing by encouraging your child to be kind.

> **Key Definition**
>
> Extrinsic motivation— something outside yourself motivating you (so in this case, some kind of external reward motivating your child to be kind again in the future)
>
> Intrinsic motivation— something inside of yourself motivating you (so the feeling inside when your child has done something kind, like pride, self-esteem, the desire to help)

LIVING IN A MATERIAL WORLD

I think that there is an enormous amount of emphasis placed on material things in our world, which adds value to "stuff" over substance. This is one of the reasons why kindness, in my opinion, is so vital. It directly opposes the consumer-drive world we live in by focusing on internal qualities and what we can give back to others in our community, rather than what we can take. If you are only taking one thing away from this chapter, please let it be the de-emphasis of physical or material rewards. Of all the rewards, this is the least effective, in part because "stuff" loses its uniqueness once you have given it. So material things (and what they represent) only have a very short shelf life; they don't have any long-term impact on behavior change (e.g., moving toward kindness) and they may undo your intentions of trying to promote kindness in your child.

PRAISE VERSUS ACKNOWLEDGMENT

Praise is another strategy that parents use when they want to reinforce a behavior; it seems like a logical conclusion and allows us to recognize kindness we see in our children—"Good on you, Little Johnny. I'm so proud of you for helping that lady cross the road!" Although not a physical reward, praise can easily become an external motivator, too. It makes your child feel good when you acknowledge their selfless act, or their good deed. Your child might come to rely on the lovely feelings of someone complimenting them in order to motivate them to do kind deeds. Okay . . . I hear you asking, *Well, what on earth can I do to try and promote and reinforce kindness in my child if I can't reward them with stuff or praise them?* You can use acknowledgments instead. So, what is the difference? And why is it important?

- Praise—a description of an action/behavior (usually the thing you want to reinforce) + a judgment (or value). "I saw

114

you playing at recess with your friend, you were such a good boy/girl." By adding a judgment (you were such a good boy/girl), you are encouraging your child to become reliant on your praise.

- Acknowledgement—a description of the action/behavior only. "I saw you playing at recess with your friend."

If you have been clear about what your expectations are (in relation to kindness), then a simple acknowledgment or thank-you is enough to reinforce the behaviors you would like to see again from your child. By adding the "judgment" or comments about the value of a particular behavior, you are reducing the opportunity for your child to assess and assign a value to their own attitudes and choices. Because the decision to be kind is so driven by morals and internal motivations, we don't want our children to become reliant on us to reinforce the importance of being kind.

So, have discussions with them, ask questions, and acknowledge the impact of their kindness so that they can see the positive impact of their actions and internalize this (there are some specific strategies and questions you can ask them in the next chapter). What I mean by "internalize" is that they will begin to see themselves as a kind person and it will become part of their schema or idea of themselves. This means that they will be driven to be kind and will feel fulfilled when they have acted kindly, because it upholds the values that they hold for themselves. This means they will get enough reward from these "internal" factors that they will want to keep being kind for their own sense of self-worth.

REFLECTING ON KINDNESS

Another important way of acknowledging your child's kind behavior is by getting them to acknowledge it for themselves. This is powerful, because it means that your child won't need to rely on someone (or something) external to validate that what they are doing is important, meaningful, and compassionate. So how can you do this? It's easy! Ask lots of questions that get your child thinking. Ask them to think back to their kind act and ask what made them do it. What would it have been like for the person who received their kindness? And how did it make them feel to be kind to someone else? These kinds of questions set up your child to really consider the impact of their actions and learn to acknowledge the power of being kind.

FOLLOWING EXPECTATIONS IS NOT THE SAME AS BEING KIND

We all have a role to play in the smooth running of our community. The same can be said for families. There are things that we each need to contribute to our family and home life; in my household, I do most of the cooking, my husband takes the trash out, and my toddler packs her toys away after she has played with them. You can 100 percent thank your child for contributing to the running of the house, but don't give them physical, monetary, or other materialistic rewards for simply doing what is expected of them. The expectation in every family is different: Who does what? What roles do people play in the smooth running of your household? etc. This is not to be confused with chores, which usually (but not always) come with some kind of monetary or other reward.

Set Realistic Expectations

Don't set expectations that are beyond the developmental level of your child. You want to encourage them to be kind but only within their capacity. For example, toddlers aren't very good at sharing (yet), and young children are only just learning how to be empathetic and step into someone else's shoes. In our family, our toddler is expected to share but only within her capacity as a two-year-old. For example, she isn't allowed to snatch toys or games from other people; we model and encourage her to ask to join in or ask for a turn and we also use timers to regulate sharing and teaching her to delay gratification (i.e., learning to wait for her turn and understand that sharing is reciprocal). These kinds of expectations and responsibilities should generally evolve as your child gets older. Just make sure your expectations are realistic and based on your child's capacity, skills, and developmental level. The impact of unrealistic expectations is that your child will never find enough "proof" of their kindness or other good deeds if the bar is set too high for them. This decreases their confidence, self-esteem, and self-efficacy.

RANDOM REWARDS

Although we have been exploring the impact of rewards on genuine kindness, I absolutely understand that you might want to acknowledge your child's hard work in some way. There are three key things to take into account if you want to do this:

- If you want your child to remember your appreciation of their kind deed for longer, then you could choose to pair it with some kind of rewarding experience. When you pair their kindness with a memory (which lasts longer than material stuff), this helps create a moment that really sticks out in their mind. Use this as an opportunity to spend quality time with your child; go get a hot chocolate together, play their favorite game, go to a museum or the zoo.

- Even if you follow all the recommendations previously discussed, then I would still advise you to be careful about giving rewards all of the time (even in this case, it still applies to an experience/activity). If your child comes to expect that their kind behavior comes with a prize, then it defeats the purpose of this book and mitigates your desire to encourage your child to be kind. The whole point of kindness is acting selflessly or showing generosity of spirit. If they are doing something for a reward, then it is self-serving—so don't be fooled! Keep any of these experiences/activities to a minimum and ensure that they are only offered randomly.

- Don't offer the reward of an activity or an experience directly after your child has done something kind. They need to feel the power and impact of their behavior, but later in the week, or later that day, you might take them aside to acknowledge their kindness, tell them that you noticed what they did (using the principles of acknowledging rather than praising), and that you want to share a hot chocolate together to appreciate them.

KINDNESS IS CATCHING

I suppose that this is one of the tricky elements about "teaching" kindness to your child; it isn't about "external" stuff that is easy to access or easy or provide. Instead, it is mostly about helping them experience and understand the power of true kindness, which is a selfless act to benefit another person (or persons).

So how can you reward your child's kindness in indirect, non-materialistic, random ways? One key way is by encouraging them to seek out kindness in other people and in different areas of their lives. If your child witnesses kind acts, they are also in a position to see the impact of this kindness on another person. Seeing the impact firsthand can be incredibly powerful and emotional and has learning opportunities that we as parents couldn't ever hope to set up intentionally. I worked with a ten-year-old girl many years ago who spoke to me about an act of kindness she had witnessed at school. On the playground, she noticed another child playing by herself. We had a discussion about how this other young girl might have been feeling, and my client gave some very empathetic responses: sad, worried, and lonely. As she was watching, she saw a boy join the other young girl and told her he had noticed she was playing by herself and invited her to join him while he sorted some of his collectible cards (I forget which, but they were some kind of collectible "buzz" toy that all the kids were clambering to own at the time). I asked my client why she thought the boy was inviting the girl to play. How would it have felt being invited to play if that other girl had initially been feeling sad, worried, and lonely? This was a great learning opportunity that came from witnessing a random act of kindness. My young client was able to see the power of "noticing" others and being compassionate to their needs and emotions. Without any prompting, she reported back to me in our session the following week that she had gone searching for lonely kids in the playground to join her with her jump rope. Witnessing that act of kindness had affected her in a profound way and made her consider and change her own behaviors to replicate the kindness she had seen.

This brings me to my very long and involved point: that kindness is catching. So, by getting our children to notice and acknowledge the power of kindness that other people display, they are also likely to "catch the bug" and replicate those acts of kindness. James Fowler and Nicholas Christakis[8] conducted an interesting study on this very concept. They used a "Public Goods Game," which is a research activity where participants are given a number of tokens (representing money) and were allowed to put as many or as few tokens as they wish in a public pot, which is then shared among everyone at the end of the game. At the end of the game, they also got to keep any tokens that they didn't put in the public pot. Their research found that if even one person put some tokens into the public pot, the others who received their share of these "public tokens" were more likely to put some of their own tokens into the public pot next time the game was played. The researchers were able to identify that kindness is a social contagion that, when felt or witnessed, is catching and can cascade through people's social networks.

So how is this a reward? you ask. Well, it is an emotional reward, not one of the materialistic rewards I warned you about.

KINDNESS IS ITS OWN REWARD (THE SCIENCE OF KINDNESS)

As human beings, we are meant to exist in groups, we are profoundly social, and kindness is one element that ensures the survival of our species. Kindness and altruism are needed because these allow people within the same group to put aside their own needs for the success of the group. Kindness is an adaptive and important part of being a human, and as such, our bodies and brains were built with structures and subsequent abilities that help us to empathize and give compassion to others. This includes our ability to use language and communicate our senses (which help us pick up and identify emotions and behaviors of other people) as well as our capacity to feel and recognize emotions in other people.

These things all allow us to understand and respond to the experience of other people, which is a core ability that underpins kindness. Everything in our body serves some kind of purpose; we have eyelashes to protect our eyes, we have hair in our nostrils to filter dirt and germs, etc. So, from this, we can tell that being altruistic is adaptive and necessary to the survival of humans. If it wasn't necessary, those skills/abilities wouldn't exist.

We also know how essential altruism is to humans because of what happens in our brains when we are kind. Basically, the brain rewards the behaviors associated with kindness and compassion in order to try and get us to keep doing it. Think of it as getting a chocolate bar every time you do something right; the chocolate bar is nice, so you keep doing that "thing" in order to get another chocolate. It's our brain's way of trying to get us to repeat behaviors that are good for us socially and emotionally. While your child might not be old enough to understand the science behind kindness, they will certainly be able to appreciate the reward of how good it feels to be kind. But for all of you who want to know why being kind feels so good, here is some science that explains why:

- Being kind actually makes people happier and improves their self-esteem and sense of optimism,[9, 10] not only from the sense of fulfilment that comes from being kind and the reward of doing a good deed, but engaging in acts of kindness creates a sense of "emotional warmth" as the body releases the feel-good hormone oxytocin.

- Kindness also has a positive effect on the people around us. This is again due to the release of oxytocin, which is released in those who witness kind acts and coincidentally makes them more likely to "pay it forward" themselves.
- Oxytocin aids physical health by lowering blood pressure. If you want to get all "science-y," this is because oxytocin causes the release of a chemical called nitric oxide, which is known to dilate blood vessels. This in turn reduces blood pressure.
- When you are kind to someone, the pleasure centers in the brain light up. This experience is often called "the helpers high."
- Serotonin is another chemical released by the body when people are kind and it makes them feel happy and helps combat stress.
- Other chemicals associated with being kind are endorphins, which are natural painkillers.
- Being kind also decreases cortisol levels in the body. Cortisol is a stress hormone also associated with prematurely aging people, so not only is kindness good for your general health, it also has antiaging properties.

Now, come on, parents—if that hasn't sold you on why kindness is important, I don't know what will?!

REFLECTION EXERCISES—REWARDING KINDNESS

1. Think about your parenting and communication style and consider what you do to try and promote or get your child to replicate particular behaviors.

2. Consider something kind you have done recently and ask yourself the same questions that you might pose to your child. What did it feel like to be kind? Why did you choose to be kind? And how might it have felt for the person(s) on the receiving your kindness?

CHAPTER 8
TIPS FOR REWARDING KINDNESS

203. Encourage your child to write anonymous "valentines" any time of year. It doesn't have to be about romantic love; their valentines could focus on showing a family member or friend how much they love and value them. Writing down their feelings helps them make their thoughts concrete, and sharing with another person will help them see how valuable their friendships/relationships are to other people.

204. Before school starts, check in with your child's classroom teacher if they need any particular supplies for the classroom. Teachers often buy supplies out of their own money, so this will benefit them and ensure your child's class has the right supplies for the

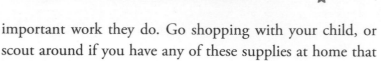
important work they do. Go shopping with your child, or scout around if you have any of these supplies at home that you would be happy to donate.

205. Work together with your child to approach local businesses to see if they have any branded stationary (pens, notepads, etc.) that they would be willing to donate to your school/classroom.

206. *As a family, start a canned-food drive in your street or neighborhood. Put up flyers, ask to have flyers put up in your local shopping center, ask neighbors/friends/family who you are close to (or on speaking terms with) if they would be willing to donate. Once you have collected the items, you can donate them to a local homeless shelter or food bank.*

207. Do a canned-food drive for cats and dogs and donate to a local pet rescue service or shelter.

208. Go for a walk as a family and set a challenge to say hello and smile to everyone you pass.

209. In the lead-up to the holidays, hook candy canes on your neighbor's windshield wipers of their cars as a surprise. Just make sure you add a note or card to increase the visibility of your candy canes—just in case they send your candy canes flying when they turn those windshield wipers on!

210. Buy a jokebook (age-appropriate, of course) or print out some jokes you have found online. Read a joke to each other every morning before school.

211. In the summer or warmer months, if you have a tradesperson or someone doing maintenance at your home, bring them some cold bottled water.

212. Get the children to help pack away the groceries when you get home from the store each week.

213. When out shopping, get ask your child to help you take the cart back (if they're old enough to do so).

214. Encourage your child to thank their friends' parents for having them over for playdates. If practiced often enough, it becomes a habit, and who doesn't want to create habits of gratitude?

215. Set a family goal for kindness. Anytime someone is kind, you can get your child to put a marble in a jar. The only trick is that someone else has to witness and verify any kind acts before a marble can be added. Arrange for a family reward once the jar is full. Try not to focus on material rewards; instead, focus on an activity you can enjoy together: going to an amusement park, getting an ice cream, going on a picnic.

216. As a family, periodically go through your cupboards and donate canned goods to a local food bank. Take this opportunity to explore that not all families have access to food and explain why it is important to give back.

217. *Create a reverse Advent calendar. On each day from the first of December, add something to a box to donate to a local homeless shelter or women's refuge. Items might include scarves, hats, gloves, deodorant, or other self-care items.*

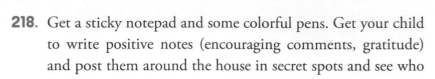

218. Get a sticky notepad and some colorful pens. Get your child to write positive notes (encouraging comments, gratitude) and post them around the house in secret spots and see who finds them.

219. *Create scenarios where they can be kind to others. For example, you might see their younger sibling reaching for a toy on a high shelf, so ask your child "Can you help your little brother grab his toy from the shelf please?" and then show appreciation if there were able to assist. Name this as an example of them demonstrating kindness.*

220. If you hear someone sneeze, say "Gesundheit" or "Bless you."

221. After dinner, have them pack their dishes into the sink or dishwasher. This can be implemented from a really early age; helping and being independent gives children a sense of accomplishment and importance. As they get older, the discussions will move toward being responsible for their own mess and showing appreciation for whoever cooked by taking their dishes to the sink and tidying the dinner table.

222. Get your child to help you bake for someone else (family, friends) and bring the goodies to them for no other reason than you want to brighten their day.

223. Rewards don't have to be objects (gifts, money, etc.). Give your child a clap, high five, or a cuddle to show your appreciation.

224. Invite a new student at their school over for a playdate. They might not necessarily understand why, but have a conversation about loneliness and see if they can understand or empathize about what it might feel like to be isolated.

225. *As a family, go to a loved one's sporting match to cheer them on. They will appreciate your presence, and it also teaches your child that encouraging and supporting someone else's success doesn't take away from their own achievements—it's not a competition!*

226. On public transportation, stands up for someone who needs the seat more than you do.

227. If you demonstrate a random act of kindness (holding open up a door, picking up spilled change/coins), and someone says thank you, use this opportunity to ask your child how it feels to do something nice for someone else.

228. If a loved one has a child (including fostering and adoption), create a care package for the new parents. Ask your child what they can think of that would be nice to include. You might bake some dinners, or prepare some snacks, or even knit/make something for the new child to welcome them. Discuss the impact of your gift and what it would feel like to receive it with your child.

229. Let someone who needs it jump in front of you in line.

230. If a new student starts at your child's school, discuss what they think it would be like to be new and what they would worry about. It will help them develop empathy for a peer who might be lonely, scared, etc.

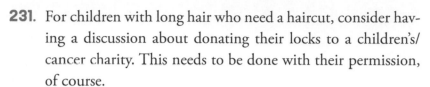

231. For children with long hair who need a haircut, consider having a discussion about donating their locks to a children's/cancer charity. This needs to be done with their permission, of course.

232. Alternatives to rewarding kind behaviors with material objects is to create a "Merit Award" for your child instead. Okay, technically this is a material object, but it's actually a memory or record of their kind deed. It will also create a sense of connection with your pride and acknowledgment of their kind behavior. The Merit Award can be decorated by your child, and it could be laminated or stuck to the fridge. Just make sure it is displayed proudly!

233. *When they are returning books to the library, sit down together and write some nice notes to slip into the pages for another child to find. Think about writing encouraging statements or kind words, like "I hope you enjoy this book as much as I did," "Happy reading," "Have an awesome day!" You can also ask your child what they would think if they got a surprise note in their book!*

234. Hold the elevator for someone if you can see they are rushing or might not make it before the door closes.

235. Sit down together and pack a backpack for a child who is in need. Ask your child about all the things that they need to be safe and happy. You could encourage them by getting them to think about food, water, warmth, clothes, their favorite teddy or comfort item, books to read, etc. Fill a backpack

with these things—it could be a mixture of new or very gently used items—and donate it to a local women's refuge or charity for children. This activity will get your child thinking empathetically. They will be considering what they need and want and applying this idea to someone who doesn't have the same things that they do. It might also be useful to talk about what it would be like for a child (similar in age or even gender to them) to receive this gift.

236. *Set up a "Kindness Scavenger Hunt" for your child to play. Make a list of people in your life that your child can show kindness to: you, siblings, extended family like grandparents, aunts, and uncles, or people in the community like neighbors or their teacher. Every time they are kind to someone on the list, they need to get proof (a photo or a letter signed by the person) before they can check it off. You can either encourage them to complete it by themselves, or you can set a challenge for your family to try and do one weekend.*

237. Sit down with your child and ask them (or get them to write down) what they think are the qualities of a good friend. Why do they think this?

238. Ask them how they demonstrate being a kind friend and encourage them to give you examples.

239. Write encouraging notes and leave them in books that you plan to donate to a local charity or sell at a garage sale. This

will give the next person reading the book a nice surprise and could really brighten their day!

240. Play the "Kind/Unkind Sorting Game." Make a list of behaviors that could be considered kind or unkind; for example, shouting, giving a hug, swearing, reading to someone, etc. Write them all down on separate pieces of card, or print out some pictures to signify the behavior. Get them to sort through the cards and put them into two separate piles "kind" and "unkind." You can target these cards to show behaviors they might be struggling with, or behaviors that you really want to emphasize are kind.

241. You can buy blank labels or stickers from most stationary or office supply stores. Spend some time with your child drawing and writing inspirational messages on them, like "You can do it!" "Have a great day" "I believe in you," etc. Then set your child a challenge to give these stickers out to friends and family. At the end of the day, check in with them to see how many they gave away and people's reactions to them.

242. Pick some flowers from your garden or purchase a small bunch. As a family, or just with your child, go to the local hospital and donate the bunch of flowers to the nurses on staff. Talk to your child about the work nurses do and explain that giving them some flowers is a great way to appreciate their work. This is a great way to expand their circle of concern as well as acknowledging the important roles that strangers play in creating the community around them.

243. *Go through your cupboards and give away any old coats to a local homeless shelter. You could also write*

some kind notes and put them in the pockets for people to find.

244. Get your child to teach you something. It could be anything; showing you how to replicate an art/craft they did in school, a song they learned on the recorder, or some kind of IT/ technology wizardry that children seem capable of! It doesn't matter what it is; helping someone else will give your child a sense of purpose and pride. It also teaches patience and good communication skills, which are both essential to being kind.

245. If you know how to knit, teach your child, if not, you can have a fun afternoon together learning from a tutorial online. Set a task to knit a scarf each and then donate them to a local homeless shelter.

246. Be very specific with your language when labeling kindness you notice in your child. You want to acknowledge that kindness is part of their identity, so instead of saying "Gee, *that* was so kind to help your friend with their homework!" say "Gee, *you* were so kind to help your friend with their homework!" It makes the connection that the kindness comes from them, not some external event or factor. Just make sure to read my section on rewarding kindness to get some idea of when it is an appropriate time to share this kind of message.

247. Create some handmade bookmarks together. They could have drawings or inspirational quotes on them. Take a bunch of these bookmarks and slip them into books at your local library or school library.

248. If you give a compliment to someone, say, for example, a really attentive shop attendant or customer service staff, ask your child what it would be like for the other person to receive that compliment. How would they feel? Why is it nice to be appreciated?

249. Teach your children the art of congratulations! To be kind, it is important to be able to appreciate the "wins" or successes of others, and not see it as directly competing or interfering with your own needs. So, try to encourage your child to give a friend a high five and say "Congratulations" if they win a competition or if a family member achieves a goal.

250. You don't necessarily have to donate any money, but clap or show some appreciation for street performers.

251. Our world needs more kindness and compassion, so spread the word and "love bomb" your neighborhood or family members with cards or letters that have an inspirational or kind message.

252. Make it a challenge for you and your child to smile at every new person you pass when you are out together (depending on the age of your child, you may want to couple this with discussions about stranger danger as appropriate). Talk to your child about the reactions you got when you smiled at people and ask them what it feels like when people smiled back or acknowledge them in some way (saying hello, waving, etc.).

253. If you are out together, take the opportunity to be kind. For example, hold a door open for a stranger. You can then ask your child questions to get them thinking about the kind action. Why did they think you held the door open? How could the other person have been feeling when you held it open?

254. Work together to make fill two toiletries bags—one for a female and one for a male—to donate to a local homeless service.

Explain that sometimes people who don't have a lot of money need to make choices and prioritize which self-care/toiletries they are going to buy because they often cannot afford to get them all. Give someone the gift of dignity by filling a bag with (new) essential items. So, for men it might be a razor, face cream, lip balm, hair ties, toothbrush, toothpaste, shampoo, deodorant, etc. And for women, some examples might be; sanitary products, shampoo, conditioner, hairbrush, face cream, sunblock. Any of those daily items that we can take for granted.

255. *As a family, make a dog toy (a rope or chew toy) and donate it to a local animal/dog shelter.*

256. If your child is older, arrange to do some volunteering at your local animal shelter together. They often need helpers to clean out stalls/crates and play with or walk the animals. You can talk through what is feels like to help and be kind to these animals.

257. Brainstorm, as a family, what you can do together as an act of kindness. Let everyone contribute and either vote or go through with all the suggestions. Plan a weekend or a day of kindness where you implement these plans. Remember, it doesn't have to be big or expensive to be kind.

258. Get a notebook and some fancy pens (different colors, glittery, scented, etc.). There is something enticing about new stationery and a blank notebook that motivates us to fill it! This is a book for your family to record your random acts of kindness. Leave it in a spot where everyone can access it and encourage the entire family to add entries that include dates and details of their random acts of kindness. Not only will this allow your child to see his/her family demonstrating

kind behaviors, but they will also want to fill in the book themselves to use those fancy pens and join in the activity with their family.

259. Set a kindness challenge (this may or may not have a reward, just pay close attention to my comments about what an appropriate reward for kindness might look like). Set them a challenge to express two kind acts and to record three kind acts that they have witnessed.

260. *Encourage your kids to turn off lights and electronic equipment (TV, microwaves, laptop chargers, etc.) when not in use. You can couple this with a discussion about the impact of electricity on the environment as well as the cost of using electricity. You don't want to shoulder your child with feeling responsible for the family bills, but they do need to feel responsible for their usage.*

261. Go to a secondhand store or garage sale and find a piece of furniture to reclaim and restore together. You don't need a lot of skill; usually being able to sand (hand sanding, not machine) and paint will suffice. This helps the environment as you are reducing waste and you can have the added bonus of teaching your child the value of recycling.

262. Periodically go through your cupboards and donate your old towels and blankets to your local animal shelter. Depending on the age of your child, you could take them with you to see the pets/animals that your donation will be benefiting.

263. As your children get older, they won't be as interested in their old books, either because their tastes change or they mature and need new challenges. So, work together and go through their bookshelf to see if there are any books that they don't read anymore (still in good condition) that could be donated to their school library.

264. It might be nice to have a project that involves making a soft toy, whether it be sewing, knitting, or if your resources (or time constraints) stretch, then possibly buying a new teddy or soft toy. The project will ensure some valuable quality time together, but you can also donate the soft toy to a women's shelter for other children to have. Depending on their age or developmental level, you could couple this with discussions about why some families might not be able to live together or why some children don't have their own toys to play with or hug.

265. Work together on a project to grow plants or wildflowers that particularly attract native wildlife, butterflies, and bees to your garden. Not only are you making the garden pretty, but you are helping feed and care for the animals in your area.

266. Get children to write (or draw a picture) a get-well card and send it to a loved one who is unwell.

267. Go to a family member or friend's concert or play. Cheer and clap to show your appreciation of their hard work. Check in with your child and see what they think or how they would feel if their loved ones came to support them in similar circumstances.

268. Periodically, go through your child's room or toy box and remove any old toys that they don't play with and donate

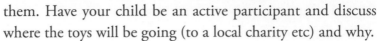

them. Have your child be an active participant and discuss where the toys will be going (to a local charity etc) and why.

269. Each season, sort through their clothes and donate any clothes still in good condition to a local charity. Do this activity together, and you can even model going through your own clothes. It will be a chance to connect as you speak with them about why you are donating the clothes.

270. *One night a week, encourage a rule that your child picks what the family will be having for dinner and helps make it. As an added bonus, you can spend some quality time together going over recipes or searching the Internet for inspiration. As your child gets older, they can have more responsibility for how much involvement they have in the task. Younger children will just enjoy having a say and helping in the kitchen, while adolescents will be learning life skills and feeling independent when they are able to make an entire meal for the family. However, more importantly, looking after their family (by nourishing them) will help your child feel the effects of being kind.*

271. After playing a game, playing with toys etc., they should clean up after themselves. Even young children learn quickly to pack away their toys if they are encouraged. What starts as enjoyment and pleasure from being thanked and appreciated

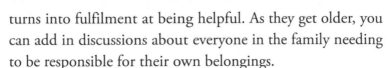

turns into fulfilment at being helpful. As they get older, you can add in discussions about everyone in the family needing to be responsible for their own belongings.

272. From an early age, give your child chores (making sure that they are developmentally and age-appropriate). There shouldn't necessarily be a reward for doing the chores; it is simply about the roles and duties that everyone needs to perform in order to keep a family and household functioning.

273. Collect small coins/denominations to place in a jar (money left over from shopping, or other small purchases). Have the jar or container in a prominent place in the house and get your child to decorate the jar, or a find a protector to stand near the jar (like a dinosaur, toy, drawing, etc.) to keep the money safe. Once the jar is full, have a discussion about what you will do with the money. Purchase school supplies to donate? Buy jars of food to donate? A donation straight to a charity of choice? Let your child take the lead on this and explore why they have made their particular choice.

274. Buy or make some bubble mixture, put the mix into a jar with a bubble wand (you can make one easily with a pipe cleaner if you don't want to buy plastics or cannot afford to purchase this new). Get your child to write a note with either kind words, wishing someone a nice day or hopes that someone is enjoying their day. Attach the note to the bubble mixture, take your child to a park, and leave it for another family to find and enjoy.

275. As a family, make snacks for animals and donate them to a local animal shelter. Do some research to make sure these are healthy and safe snacks.

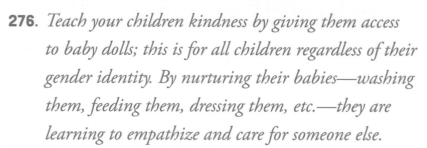

276. *Teach your children kindness by giving them access to baby dolls; this is for all children regardless of their gender identity. By nurturing their babies—washing them, feeding them, dressing them, etc.—they are learning to empathize and care for someone else.*

277. Provide dress-up clothes for your child that give them an opportunity to explore empathy in different roles. Think about getting a fireman's uniform, nurses' and doctors' medical kits (plastic of course!), a vet bag, etc. It allows them to use their imagination and explore roles or characters that demonstrate compassion and empathy as part of their job (e.g., looking after others).

278. Taking on a pet is a huge responsibility for your child, and the entire family. So please don't take this step lightly. However, if you are thinking about getting a pet, it is a very good way to teach your child about caring for and considering the needs of others, as they will have to think about walking, grooming, feeding, and giving water to their pet. If you aren't ready to take on a pet (and there is no pressure to do so), see if you can find an alternate way to still instill this sense of accountability. You might think about temporarily fostering a pet from a local shelter, helping a neighbor walk their dog, or even getting your child something like sea monkeys or a hermit crab (pets that are generally low allergen and permissible in rental homes). If pets really aren't your thing, think about a plant that your child can nurture.

279. Help your child plan a teddy bear drive at their school. Encourage other students to bring in teddy bears that can then be donated to local hospitals or police departments who can share the teddies with children in need.

280. When a loved one has a birthday, sit with your child and write little love notes for them. Put all the notes into a jar and decorate it to give to them on their birthday.

281. World Read Aloud Day is on February 1. If your child is old enough to read to you, pick some books to read aloud together. If your child is younger, you can simply allocate some time to read to them. This is important quality time that you are spending together, but reading aloud is also a selfless act of kindness for another person. (This can be implemented any and every day, of course.)

282. If you have an older child, discuss whether they might like to be part of a mentoring program (like a Big Brother or Big Sister kind of setup). It will give them the opportunity to give back and see how good it feels to give their time and compassion.

283. If your child is an adolescent or is a mature child, you might consider doing some volunteering together. It could be through a local community or religious group. Ask them their preferences and whether there is any issue or social problem they would like to support (animal welfare, home-lessness, etc.) and see if you can find any opportunities to do some volunteering as a family.

284. Create a kindness calendar and place it in a prominent place (on the fridge, on your child's bedroom door, etc.). Together, you can print a calendar from the Internet or draw your own calendar for the month. Encourage your child to write down and record one kind act they did each day and review their completed calendar together at the end of the month. If you

child isn't writing yet, then have the discussion and you can help them write it down. At the end of the month, discuss what it feels like seeing all the positive things they have done and think about the impact it might have had on other people. Also, you might ask them how they feel after seeing a month of kind acts.

285. Find some time to spend with your child and research some inspiring quotes on kindness. You can either print some pictures to go along with them, or create your own artwork together, but display the finished products around the house. It will remind your entire family of what inspires and motivates you to be a kind person.

286. Start a tradition in your family of giving the gift of presence . . . not presents. Instead of focusing on material goods, you can try and give the gift of an experience, time together, essentially any activity that you can enjoy together.

287. Paint some rocks with inspirational quotes and hide them (but not too well) around your neighborhood for other people to find. On one side of the rock, write/paint the hashtag #bekindeveryday with a quick message asking people to upload pictures of their rock and where they found it to try and connect with other people who are spreading the message of kindness.

288. If your child notices a peer in the playground is lonely or seems to play by themselves, encourage them to invite them over for a play date. Depending in their age or developmental level, you might want to talk about what it feels like to be lonely or scared.

289. Encourage your child to notice others who are lonely at recess or lunch (at school) and invite them to come and join in the games/conversation.

290. Extend the previous tip and ask them what it would feel like for the other child if someone noticed they were lonely and invited them to join in. These sorts of questions help improve their sense of empathy and connection with the experiences of others.

291. Pack an extra piece of fruit or a snack for them to take to school and share with a classmate who didn't bring lunch.

292. Get crafting and create a voucher book for them to fill with kind gestures, like "Give a compliment," "Help someone out with a chore," etc. The vouchers are to be used by anyone in the family to ask for help (practical or emotional help). Negotiate with your family what the vouchers might contain, but essentially you want them to be in line with your values as a family. So, the vouchers might focus on teamwork or respect.

CHAPTER 9

EXPANDING YOUR CHILD'S CIRCLE OF CONCERN

M ost people are hard-wired to be empathetic, which is a skill that allows us to step into another person's shoes and understand what they are feeling. It's easier for children to be kind to people they know, as they can see the impact of their actions, but the difficulty is getting children to expand their "circle of concern" and include other people who are outside their immediate family and friendship group. We all exist within a series of circles that increase in size; we are at the center of our world (a small little bubble), that circle is surrounded by another circle filled with our immediate family and friends, and a wider circle around that filled with people in our wider community. This chapter focuses on how we can help our children build empathy by getting outside their comfort zone, exploring differences, and expanding their concern—moving them outside their own little bubble where they focus only on getting their own needs met to being aware of and concerned for others in wider circles surrounding them.

PLACING PEOPLE ON THEIR RADAR

Children are empathetic and kinder toward people they know, so it's up to parents to help their children notice and consider people who are outside their own "circles." You can do this by helping them see how others might be feeling or experiencing a situation. Initially, it might be easier to find others who are similar to them (e.g., children of the same age or gender, or students at the same school) and get them to do a bit of detective work. Help them point out similarities and differences that they have with groups of people. Ask them who is in their group, and why? What are their similarities and differences? And who is not in their group and why? And what are the similarities and differences with these individuals? It is important for children to notice and be aware of their own preferences and bias for belonging to particular groups, but they also need to be equally aware of who they don't naturally gravitate toward or include.

I recall working with a family with a teenage daughter who was bullying other girls in her grade. She was not a bad person by any stretch of the imagination; at the core of it, she struggled to tolerate differences because she saw them as frightening/threatening and she was egocentric. Egocentrism is not a criticism—we are all in some ways egocentric—however, these two issues coupled resulted in bullying behavior in this particular young lady. Our sessions together focused on games and activities that got her stepping outside her circle (and comfort zone) and into someone else's shoes and learning to tolerate differences. I also worked closely with her mom and dad to implement family events and discussions to reinforce the work we were doing in session (many of these tips are included in the next chapter). These activities were aimed at increasing her knowledge and acceptance of others, as well as reflecting on the impact of her own behavior on others. By building on these two areas, she was able to increase her sense of empathy, which resulted in less conflict and more stable friendships.

START BEING ACTIVE

There are different ways to practice kindness. One way to be kind is to open your eyes and be active when you see people in need. Do you notice when people could use a helping hand? A sense of community is created when people are kind to those in need. Opening your eyes means noticing when others are suffering; however, it is easy to be "unaware" of discrimination when it isn't happening to us, or conversely, when we feel powerless to change anything. Children naturally feel a sense of distress when they see or hear about inequality or suffering. So, take advantage of this natural compassion and harness it in order to instill a drive to be kind rather than teaching them to accept the status quo. We need to encourage our children to become aware of bias and how it impacts their desire to be kind to all people, not just people in their group.

To address bias and stereotyping, it is important to ask your child lots of questions and also be prepared to answer lots of questions as a parent. Generally, bias comes from preferring your own social group or finding connection with those you are similar to;

however, it doesn't take a lot for this preference for similarity to become discrimination. As our children grow up, they become increasingly concerned with figuring out who they are and where they fit in the world. If you want to encourage your child to be kind, they must have an understanding of difference and acknowledge or know which groups they automatically align with. It's not that you can stop your child from being biased toward connecting with a particular group—that is human nature, but the important part is helping them become aware of their personal bias in order to build tolerance and acceptance toward other groups of people outside their circle of concern.

So how can we do this? Get them outside their comfort zone, not in any way that will expose them to danger, but in a way that exposes them to differences. Different ways of living, different status or roles in the community, different ways that people look, act, think, and believe. By taking them out of their comfort zone, you not only give them an opportunity to reflect and be grateful for what they have, but also give them perspective and an understanding of what it is like for people who might be different than them. This helps build empathy, which is a key element of kindness.

It's Okay to Talk about Uncomfortable Things

It's important to talk to our children about those who are different than them in order to dispel myths and incorrect ideas. We want our children to become tolerant, which is essentially having an attitude that is open to and respectful of difference, whether that be ethnic, religious, gender, mental, or physical differences. Being tolerant means that your child will see difference as something valuable, something to learn from, and it will help them reject stereotypes or discrimination, oppose prejudice, and discover common ground with other people.

Children internalize what they know about themselves (for example, how they look, how they sound, their abilities and status in the community) and they are naturally wary of others who are different. As we want to build tolerance, which is an accepting and kind way of thinking and acting toward others, we cannot shy away from these differences. In order to help our children be kind, we need to encourage them to think and care about other people regardless of how similar or different others might be from them.

Children don't really have a filter until they get a bit older. They can be quite cutting or unintentionally rude in their comments without intending to . . . which can be mortifying as their parent. At some point in your journey as a parent, I'm sure most of you have wanted the ground to open and swallow you up. I must have heard dozens (okay, more than dozens) of stories from parents whose children asked them quite loud and often embarrassing questions about people in their vicinity. The questions were not meant to be embarrassing, their child was simply curious, but the parents described feeling as though their questions were intrusive or rude because they were centered around the differences a child had noticed: "Daddy, how come that lady is in a wheelchair?" "Mummy, why is that man asking for money?" "What's wrong with that person over there?" These questions only become shameful or embarrassing if we make them so.

It is too easy to blush, shush your child, and whisper that it's not polite while you drag them out of earshot. We think we are teaching our children to be kind by getting them to ignore differences, but this doesn't change the fact that they notice difference—or that difference does exist between people. All we are teaching them when we shush them is that difference is something to be ashamed of. So next time your child has a question, don't avoid it; take the opportunity to talk it through with them. The next chapter will outline some specific activities you can try in response to potentially awkward questions and encourage your child to see similarities rather than differences.

REFLECTION EXERCISES—EXPANDING YOUR CHILD'S CIRCLE OF CONCERN

1. Ask yourself how you treat and engage with people you consider to be different than you. Is it the same or different than how you treat people you consider to be the same or similar to yourself?

2. Which people are in your circles? And which people aren't in your circles? Why?

3. Without any judgment, think about someone or a group of people that you are curious about. What questions would you ask them and why do you want to know? This particular reflection might help you to see that it's normal that your child is curious about things, because adults are just as curious.

CHAPTER 10

TIPS FOR EXPANDING YOUR CHILD'S CIRCLE OF CONCERN

◇◇◇◇◇◇◇◇◇◇◇◇◇◇◇◇◇◇◇◇◇◇◇◇◇◇◇◇◇◇◇◇◇◇◇◇

293. Friendship Day is celebrated on July 30. Encourage your child to think about something kind they could do to appreciate their best friend. It could be writing them a letter, drawing a picture, or baking their favorite treat.

294. Create some hug coupons for your family. Anyone in your household can tear off a coupon and get a hug from another.

295. During a car trip, allocate a set time frame to allow each person to pick the radio station or music being played. Any complaints during someone else's choice gets a minute (or some other prenegotiated amount) taken off the timer when it's their turn. Not only will everyone get to have their own preferences considered, but when it's not their turn, they learn about the turn taking and self-sacrifice that are required in a group setting.

296. *Set a timer for turn taking. If you have multiple children who aren't good at sharing, or there is some kind of social event where your child and others are bickering over the use of one particular toy/game/ piece of equipment, set a timer. That way everyone gets a turn, and your child learns about turn taking, patience, and delaying gratification.*

297. Set up family movie night once per week. Every member of the family takes a turn to plan the evening (including what snacks to bring/make and what movie to watch—the only rule is that it's appropriate for all family members to join). The age of your child will impact the level of autonomy they have here. Essentially, you want your child to start planning and thinking about arranging something for the family to enjoy together, but they also learn gratitude and appreciation when it's someone else's turn to go to the effort of planning, or learn to compromise (if they don't particularly like the movie or the food being arranged), which is essential to being kind.

298. Ask them to help write in birthday cards for family and friends (if they are younger, they can draw a picture). It is a way of showing love and that they are thinking about someone else and wishing positive things for them.

299. Find them a pen pal. There are lots of websites and places where children can sign up to be pen pals. You could even ask their classroom teacher to point you in the direction of a safe and reputable organization. Having a pen pal will allow them an opportunity to learn more about another person (showing compassion and good communication skills) and is also a lot of fun. Who doesn't like receiving a handwritten letter in the mail?!

300. *Make a bird feeder together as a project. Not only will your child reap the emotional rewards from a sense of completion and pride, but they will be helping feed and care for wildlife in your area.*

301. Celebrate Earth Day (April 22) by decorating a flowerpot together, or each member of the family can decorate their own pot and then plant some seedlings. It is also a prime opportunity to talk about sustainability, the benefits of having plants around, and the role of trees/plants in processing and removing carbon dioxide from the air.

302. In many cities, Earth Hour is celebrated by turning off electric lights for one hour (it changes every year but is usually at the end of March). You can light some candles or set up torches and enjoy some family time but also discuss the benefits of using less electricity on the environment.

303. Teach them to knit or crochet (or find a good YouTube channel if you aren't particularly adept). Over a period of time, support them while they work on a big project, such as a blanket to donate to your local hospital.

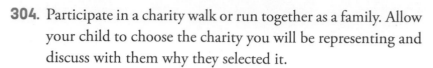

304. Participate in a charity walk or run together as a family. Allow your child to choose the charity you will be representing and discuss with them why they selected it.

305. *It is perfectly okay if your child notices differences between themselves and another person. What you don't want to do is turn that into a judgment or comparison. So, don't shut down their questions or comments; simply reframe and ask them to look for similarities. You might get them to consider what they have in common by asking "Do you both have a nose?" "Are your clothes similar?" "Are you close in age?" "Do you both have a hat on?"*

306. To help your child learn that physical differences don't actually make people different or scary, take them to your local pet store or zoo. One really good example is to look at the fish; they come in huge varieties of colors, sizes, and shapes. Ask your child how they know they are fish. They will usually answer that they know they are a fish because they live in water, have fins, gills, tails, etc. You can then add in a discussion at this point about how humans are the same as fish (well, not really, but stick with me!). We might look a little different on the outside, but there are certain things that make us all human (or the same species). You could also save the learning opportunity for some time in the future where they ask you about or notice differences in the physical appearance of another person. Remind them about the time you went to the pet store and looked at all the different fish.

307. Notice opportunities to help your neighbors. Offer to walk their dog, shovel snow, or rake leaves from their path, take their trash out if they have forgotten. Encourage your child to join in and see if they can identify any opportunities to show random acts of kindness.

308. Inspire your child to write a letter or draw a picture and send it to another child who is sick or who has a sibling that is sick. There are many professional services around the world that link or promote this kind of "pen pal" system. Or they could write/draw something to be sent to a local children's hospital. The point is to encourage empathy and awareness of others' plight and experiences that may differ from their own.

309. Plan a street party to get your neighbors together. It creates a sense of community and an opportunity to expand your child's circle of concern.

310. On World Environment Day (June 5), take some bags and protective gear and clear your local park, beach, etc. of trash. Remember to be safe and only move/touch rubbish you can openly see using the right equipment (tongs, gloves, etc.).

311. Pick some flowers from your garden. Work with your child to make them into a pretty bouquet, write a heartfelt note together, and give it to a friend just because.

312. Travel! If you can't travel far (due to finances or other life circumstances), then immerse your family in another culture or country (think food, clothing, music, pictures, etc. to set the scene). When learning to be kind, it's important to understand perspective and how other people experience things. Travel or being exposed to these differences can take them

outside their comfort zone and expose them to new ideas and challenge them (in a good way) to see things differently.

313. Read books about different cultural holidays or traditions. Even if you have a religion that your family practices, it's important to teach tolerance by educating your child about what others believe. As they grow up, they will be exposed to different beliefs, and it's important to teach them about these differences in a respectful way and instill curiosity and interest, rather than fear or judgment.

314. Spend some time in your garden picking flowers with your child. Ask them to think of a person they know who would really appreciate the flowers (e.g., someone who needs a bit of a pick-me-up). It could be a friend/peer or an adult in their life, like their teacher or a family member. Create a small bouquet, or it could even just be an individual flower with a kind and encouraging note tied to it. Anonymously deliver the flower(s) to the person in need. You can add even more to this activity by asking your child what it might feel like to receive such a kind gift? Or if they are younger, you could narrate and tell them what it would mean to someone: "Wow, those flowers were so pretty! I'm sure your uncle will feel really happy when he sees them!"

315. If there are any bugs in your house, show kindness and compassion by taking them back outside. Ask your child to tell you if they see any bugs so you can work together to help them get back outside. I do need to stress not to pick up any venomous/poisonous bugs and ensure that your child is also aware of this rule, or create a limit that they should always call you first to check in about bug-removal duties.

316. Give your child the opportunity to play and engage with groups of people (or other children) who are different from them. Think about enrolling them in playgroups, child-care facilities, sporting groups, etc. that have a diverse population.

317. If your family follows a particular religion, involve your children in the practices, traditions, and community. It can instill a sense of pride in them, as well as the opportunity to build connections with others. If you don't have a particular religion, focus on your values as a family (immediate and extended), and discuss the importance of these values as well as what you do as a family to uphold them.

318. If you don't follow a particular religion, or if you are willing, ask a close friend or extended family member who follows a (different) religion to teach you and your child about a special holiday or religious celebration. Understanding builds acceptance and tolerance.

319. Play the "Circle of Concern" game. Draw three circles: one small circle, then a bigger circle around the first one, and then a final, bigger circle surrounding the other two (think of it like an onion, circles within circles). In the center circle, write your child's name, or if they are very young, print a picture or draw a picture of them. Then work together to fill in the next circle, which is all about people who are in their immediate life (family, friends, etc.). The widest circle is for people in the community who they may or may not have direct contact with: think about their teachers, local community groups, librarians, friends of friends, etc. If your child is old enough, you can ask them questions, like:

- Which groups do they belong to?

- How do you know that they belong to these groups?
- Who have we forgotten to include? Or why aren't certain people in your group?
- What would it be like for the people who haven't been included in your circles (i.e., the people being left out)?

320. Take the "Circle of Concern" game a bit further. Encourage your child to greet and say hello to people they have forgotten or didn't include in their inner circles.

321. Sit down with your child and ask them what it would be like if they increased their circle of concern? Would it be easy or hard? What would the impact be on the people they are including? You can simplify it for younger children by focusing on their school playground rather than bigger/community groups. Ask them who in the playground doesn't play with many other kids? What it would be like if someone invited that child to join in a game?

322. Demonstrate respect for the earth and pick up litter if you see it.

323. *Recycle and talk about the damage waste does to the planet. Encourage your child to help you sort out household waste for recycling. You can explore kindness to the planet and future generations depending on the age of your child.*

324. Think about upcycling old household goods to limit waste. Repurpose them or resell them.

325. Have a garage sale and donate the proceeds to a charity. Discuss with your child what charity they would like to donate to and why.

326. Find stories or nonfiction books that explore a variety of themes like kindness, friendship, etc. Take some time to explore your child's feelings and thoughts when reading the story. Ask them if they connect with any of the characters or scenarios.

327. Have a spring clean and sort through your belongings as a family. Consider recycling, reselling, and donating. You can have a discussion with your child about the meaning of "stuff" or materialism (for the older kids) and how we don't need "things" to be happy. It's also important to explore your position if you are fortunate enough to be able to donate or give away things you don't need any more.

328. If you have an older child (who is in good health), do the ration challenge or the forty-hour famine. It is a fund-raising challenge that shows people what it is like to survive on rations that refugees and people in developing countries have access to. It not only creates an opportunity to raise funds and awareness, but also gives your child a direct experience of what everyday life is like for people around the world who don't have access to the same opportunities and quality of life you do.

329. Enroll in a CPR/first-aid course as a family.

330. If your child has a younger sibling or friend, encourage them to share their knowledge or skills if the other person is struggling with something (like kicking a ball or learning their multiplication tables). It is a powerful skill to learn to help others (in a kind way, not a bragging or self-important way). Get them to talk through steps or how they learned to do something and try to get them to add in some encouraging words!

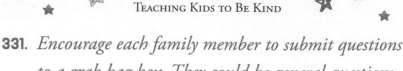

331. *Encourage each family member to submit questions to a grab bag box. They could be general questions or random things they want to know, or questions for other family members. Use these questions to start conversations during a family meeting or over dinner. This creates intentional interest in other people, which helps children to combat natural egocentrism.*

332. Encourage your child to do a charity event for a cause, like a readathon, five-kilometer walk, etc. Allow them to pick the charity and ask friends, family, and community members to donate to their cause. You could also do the charity event together as a family, using it as an opportunity to spend quality time and spread kindness together.

333. Be careful about the toys/art/books/TV shows/games you allow your children to be exposed to. Be mindful of how you and others in your family talk about people and groups or how topics are explored and ensure that they convey a message that fits with your family values.

334. If you are watching TV or reading a newspaper article and you come across stereotyping, talk this through with your children. What is a stereotype? Reinforce that not all stereotypes are true just because you see them in the media. Explore with older children the damage or negative impact that some stereotypes can have.

335. Value difference within your own family. Respect and accept that your children or extended family might have different abilities, skills, interests, and opinions. Try to avoid comparisons and value their own unique personalities and contributions to the family.

336. Avoid using words or language that promote stereotypes, even if you think your child cannot hear you or won't understand. Try to avoid jokes or name-calling even in an informal manner.

337. Try to avoid shaming your child or shutting them down if they ask questions about difference. Try to find out what they have noticed is different about someone or something, and try to explain (in the least emotive or judgmental way you can) why this difference exists. You can also ask them to try and answer their own question to see what misconceptions or ideas they might have so you can correct them. Also thank them for asking and appreciate that they want to know. Children are naturally curious and want to know all about the world around them, and we need to help them see that difference is acceptable.

338. Sometimes children don't use the gentlest language to describe differences. If your child notices or wants to talk about someone who is different to them and they ask in a public place, you could table the question to answer at another time (e.g., when you get home, or in your car). Don't shut them down, just let them know that you will answer their question later; "I can see you are really interested in why (insert topic here). Let me find out some more information and I will help you to understand later." When you are in the right space, re-affirm that it is okay to be curious and to want answers, but try and reframe what they are saying with more appropriate or acceptable language or give them an answer to their question.

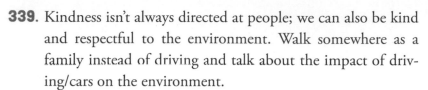

339. Kindness isn't always directed at people; we can also be kind and respectful to the environment. Walk somewhere as a family instead of driving and talk about the impact of driving/cars on the environment.

340. Celebrate Teachers Appreciation Day (October 5) by sending a kind note or handmade gift to your child's teacher. Work on it together and ask them why they are grateful for their teacher and include these reflections in the note. If they can't think, or aren't sure, you might suggest that they might be grateful for their teacher helping them to understand something, taking time to read instructions, a great sense of humor, or letting them play games.

341. Another way to show environmental kindness is by buying and encouraging the use of re-usable drink bottles (water bottles and reusable cups). Show your child some videos or talk to them about the environmental impact of single-use plastics.

342. Mark "World Kindness Day" in your calendar (November 13) and create a bit of buzz around creating kindness that day. Ask your child in advance what you can do as a family, as well as what they can do as an individual to celebrate. You could help them bake cakes for their classroom, set a challenge to smile at everyone you both see that day, etc. Get them to think up some ideas of how they can appreciate the day.

343. Celebrate International Day of Tolerance (November 16). This day is all about rejoicing difference, so think of an activity to appreciate difference in your family or community. You could bake a special meal that means something to your family or community, write down what you are grateful for, listen to or make some music that represents your community, etc.

344. *Get your child linked in with a local sports team (and encourage them to engage in a group, not individual sport). Team sports help your child learn how to work as part of a group and how to communicate and cooperate for a shared rather than independent goal.*

345. It is important to show kindness and compassion to animals as well as people. Take your child (generally this is a tip for young children) to a petting zoo and teach them about using "gentle touch." Explore how they can pat and handle animals gently and then, depending on their age, you could also explore how frightening it can be for animals to have someone pat them roughly, shout, or move quickly and unexpectedly.

346. Take them to a functioning farm. The point is to show them the effort farmers go to in order to produce food that we often take for granted because we can buy it so easily from the store. It helps them develop appreciation and also encourages them to expand their circle of concern.

347. When you go shopping, keep a bunch of reusable fabric bags to use instead of the single-use plastic bags many stores provide. You can expand on your kindness by purchasing some of the bags sold for charity (doubling the kindness is a big thumbs-up!). Also, depending on the age of your child, you might couple this decision to use reusable bags with a discussion on the impact of plastic bags on the environment.

348. For older children/adolescents, start a challenge to find at least one positive news article in the newspaper, or in a magazine. Or for younger children, cut out these articles to read to them. Find stories about everyday heroes, courageous kids, or kindness in the community.

349. Find them a mentor, someone who you think embodies kindness and compassion. Sometimes the messages from parents don't always come across the way we want them to, as it can feel a bit like nagging, or sometimes our children might switch off and not really hear what we are saying. Instead, finding them another adult or young person they can connect with and look up to, who demonstrates the values or attitudes you want to promote, can have a deep impact.

350. Once a month, have a dinner time debate using ethical dilemmas and discuss both sides of a tricky situation. One prompt might be: "Is it okay to steal food if it's to feed your starving family?" This will get your child thinking about different opinions, needs, and perspectives, which helps them learn about and tolerate difference.

351. If your neighbor, a family friend, or even your child's classmate(s) celebrate different religious holidays than your family, encourage your child to learn any traditional phrases or draw/write them an appropriate card to celebrate the day to share with the other person.

352. Challenge your child! Get them to play social detective for a day at school and find out how many classmates they have something in common with. After school, discuss their findings. Did anything surprise them? What did they have in common? This activity helps children expand their circle of concern. They are more likely to be compassionate toward

those they see as "the same" as them, so it's beneficial to encourage them to seek out similarities.

353. *Teach your child to learn to say please and thank you in another language.*

354. Research alongside your child and learn to say *hello, goodbye,* and *how are you* in another language. If you meet anyone who speaks that language, get them to put their skills to good use. This is a good way to explore differences but also show respect for those same differences.

355. Give them a high five to show your appreciation or acknowledge something awesome they have done.

356. Kids have pretty good imaginations. Use this skill to ask them to consider how their behavior might impact others. But ask really specific questions, or set up scenarios to get them thinking about how their behavior and choices impact others. "Imagine that your class is doing an art project and you decide to take all of the colored pencils and not share them. How do you think that might make other people feel?"

357. *Encourage teamwork. If your child has a friend over, or if they have a sibling, ask them to work on a project together. Ask them: "Could you both please work together and help me (insert chore or activity here, like bring the shopping in from the car, bring the dishes to the sink, etc.)?" You could also encourage them to work with you or help you out if they don't have siblings or a friend over.*

358. Get creative and come up with your family's own Appreciation Day. Pick a date in the year, or a day (e.g., the first Sunday in February) and make it an annual event that your family celebrates. Use the day as an opportunity to appreciate what you do for each other as a family. You can make it as big as you like as long as the focus is on spending some good quality time together and acknowledging the roles you all play to keep the family unit working together!

359. If your child has attended a birthday party, sit down together after the event and write the friend (and their parents) a thank-you note for the invitation. Depending on the age of your child, you might also add in a discussion about why you are thanking them; for the invitation itself, the effort they went to, to make the party enjoyable, or possibly even for a yummy party bag that they gave out at the end. Writing thank-you notes can feel old-fashioned, but people like being appreciated and acknowledged and this is a very kind habit for your child to develop.

360. In the lead-up to Christmas, many charities open up requests for gifts for children. Take your child shopping to select a brand-new toy to gift to another little boy or girl their age. This is a great opportunity to experience gratitude (that you come from a family who can afford new toys) and build their empathy (learning that not everyone has the same circumstances in life) by choosing something they would select for themselves to gift to another child who is not as fortunate. It also teaches them about the strength it takes to be selfless.

361. If your child is having a birthday party, and the whole class is not invited, don't give out invites before or during school. It's

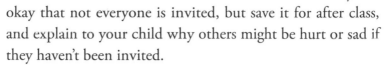

okay that not everyone is invited, but save it for after class, and explain to your child why others might be hurt or sad if they haven't been invited.

362. If you go on vacation, help or encourage your child to write a letter to a loved one back home. This is an active way to encourage them to demonstrate compassion and show that they are thinking (and maybe missing or worrying) about someone else.

363. If you have a family member or friend who is sick, work together with your child to brainstorm and create a care package for them. You can talk to your child and ask them questions about what they want to put in the care package. How do they think the person will react when they get their care package? How would they feel if they got a care package when they were sick?

364. *Grow some vegetables in your garden and donate some of your produce. This could be to friends, family, neighbors, or a local food bank or homeless service.*

365. Ask your child to find out if anyone in their class speaks another language. You could then research some phrases or words to learn so that they can speak to their classmate in another language. This demonstrates tolerance, respect, and compassion, especially for those who have learned a second language because they have moved or they need to speak it for schooling, etc.

CHAPTER 11

SUMMARY

So, there you have it! As promised . . . 365 tips to help your child learn how to be kind. The purpose of this book was to help you get into the real nitty-gritty and complexity of what it takes to be kind along with some practical tips for you to use to encourage kindness in your child. I really considered each tip carefully, as I want them to be more than just a formulaic set of rules to follow in order to develop kindness in your child. I hope that each tip prompts discussions, bringing kindness to the fore of your family's day to allow you to explore your inner workings and values as well as give your child the best opportunity to become a kind and compassionate person.

One essential element of kindness is that it shouldn't be the exception; it should form an important part of our everyday life. Children need repetition before they learn a new skill and can consistently apply or use this skill. Kindness is no exception. The tips included in this book provide you (and your child) with lots of the little moments and opportunities for learning, which will add up and give your child an understanding of what kindness looks and feels. By taking these tips on board, you are giving them the encouragement to flex their compassionate muscles every day.

I truly believe that we need more kindness in a world that makes it too easy for us to be selfish and egocentric. I think it takes much more effort and strength to be kind, and I applaud you for this passion that we share. If you weren't concerned for the morals and values of your child, you wouldn't have picked up this book and you certainly wouldn't have gotten all the way through to this final passage if you weren't driven or hopeful that, as people and a community, we can *do* better and *be* better. This is why I am so committed and enthusiastic about working with children; they are raw material that we can shape and mold, and I care intensely (like you do) about shaping them into people who see the worth of others and into people who are willing to share their good fortune, hope, and compassion. So, in a world where you can be anything, commit to helping your child choose a path of kindness. This path is one that we can walk together as individuals, families, and communities all working toward a bigger goal.

RESOURCES

◇◇

THIRTY DAYS OF GRATITUDE PROMPTS

This list of gratitude prompts is also available on my website, which includes a bit more of a rationale about why gratitude is so good for us, mentally and physically. Daily gratitude is something we can all benefit from, not just our children. If you get into a habit of expressing your appreciation, this is also something your child will internalize and recognize as important. These tips are aimed at adults but can provide great opportunities to spark conversation, modeling, and even amended gratitude prompts for your children. https://www.towardwellbeing.com/30-days-of-gratitude

1. What is something you are looking forward to?
2. What memory are you grateful for?
3. What season do you appreciate?
4. What song or piece of music do you enjoy?
5. What is a mistake that led to something positive?

6. Name one person who has had a positive impact on your life.
7. Look around you and think about what you can see (people or objects). List the things you are grateful for.
8. What season (weather) do you like the most?
9. What is something new you learned this week/month that you are grateful for?
10. What is your favorite smell?
11. Describe your favorite place in the world.
12. Which of your personality traits do you appreciate?
13. Describe a recent obstacle you have overcome.
14. Who in your life are you grateful for?
15. What about your health or body do you appreciate?
16. What is your favorite taste/food?
17. Which piece or type of technology are you most grateful for?
18. Write down the best piece of advice you have been given.
19. Describe the last kind thing you did (without being asked, or for any reward).
20. What is your favorite time of day?
21. What is something you are looking forward to this week/ month?
22. What is your favorite outfit and how does it make you feel?
23. Write down what you have done recently to look after yourself (physical or mental health).
24. What is something you can do easily, but is difficult for others?
25. Describe a time when a stranger did something nice for you.

26. What is the best gift you have ever received?
27. What traditions did you enjoy as a child or have put in place as an adult?
28. What did it feel like to fall in love for the first time?
29. Who inspires you to keep going when things are tough?
30. What is something you are really proud of?
31. (Bonus, just in case the month is thirty-one days) What is the best compliment someone has ever given you?

LIST OF EMOTIONS

You can use this list of emotions (of all intensities) to help you and your child explore different feelings! See if you can add any more to the list. You might spend some time with your child thinking about where you would put these feelings words in order of how big or how intense they feel.

Joy	Sad	Disgusted	Scared	Angry	Surprise
Happy	Devastated	Inferior	Afraid	Furious	Curious
Appreciated	Solemn	Shame	Frightened	Cross	Confused
Ecstatic	Discouraged	Guilt	Worried	Defensive	Shocked
Jolly	Gloomy	Ignored	Insecure	Frustrated	Interested
Glad	Miserable	Embarrassed	Nervous	Outraged	Incredulous
Thankful	Lonely	Inadequate	Anxious	Annoyed	Mystified
Optimistic	Disappointed	Unaccepted	Terrified	Insulted	Thoughtful

NOTES AND FURTHER RESEARCH

1. Hawkley, L. C., & Cacioppo, J. T. (2003). Loneliness and pathways to disease. *Brain, Behavior, and Immunity.* 17 (1). 98–105.
2. Matthew, T., Danese, A., Caspi, A., & Fisher, H. L. (2019). Lonely young adults in Britain: Findings from an epidemiological cohort study. *Psychological Medicine, 49* (2). 268–277.
3. http://ei.yale.edu/ruler/ruler-overview/.
4. Eckman P. https://www.paulekman.com/resources /universal-facial-expressions/.
5. Mischel, W., et al. (1989). Delay of gratification in children. *Science*, 244(4907), 933–938.
6. American Psychological Society. https://www.apa.org /helpcenter/willpower-gratification.pdf

7. Roth, G., Kanat-Maymon, Y., & Bibi, U. (2010). Prevention of school bullying: The important role of autonomy-supportive teaching and internalization of pro-social values. *British Journal of Educational Psychology*, retrieved from http://selfdeterminationtheory.org/SDT/documents/2010_RothKanat-MaymonBibi_bullying_BJEP.pdf.

8. Fowler, J.H., & Christakis, N. A. (2010). Retrieved from https://www.pnas.org/content/early/2010/02/25/0913149107

9. Harvard Health Publishing (2011). Retrieved from https://www.health.harvard.edu/newsletter_article/in-praise-of-gratitude.

10. Otake, K., Shimai, S., Tanaka-Matsumi, J., Otsui, K., & Fredrickson, B. L. (2006). Happy people become happier through kindness: A counting kindness intervention. *Journal of Happiness Studies, 7,* (3). 361–375. Retrieved from: https://www.ncbi.nlm.nih.gov/pmc/articles/PMC1820947/.

ACKNOWLEDGMENTS

I would like to take this opportunity to acknowledge and thank my parents. Thank you, Mum, for being the ideas woman, my rock, for supporting me no matter what and never failing to give the best advice. Dad, thank you for your humor and for always telling me how proud you are, as well as my memory for retaining random facts.

To Linda, thank you for being steadfast in your support and believing in me. And Steve, thank you for your patience and deciding to stick around even after Kalgoorlie.

I also want to acknowledge my siblings; Gail, Sali, Michelle, Vicki, Naomi, and Jacob. My family means everything to me, and you were the first people to teach me about kindness and compassion and set me up with the values that drive me.

I would also like the thank the people who have come into my life: my husband, Jason, who is unendingly supportive and makes me believe in myself; my daughter, Marni, who is my reason for writing this book (because

I want the world she is growing up in to be filled with kindness); and for my extended family—Jeff, Jan, Rachel, and Cai—who have accepted me into their lives from day one and made me feel at home.

To the best group of friends a girl could ask for; Channy, Gem, Zoe, Rhi, Kirsty, Kim and Sarah, we have been through thick and thin and I cant thank you enough for always being in my corner.

I am so appreciative of my critique partner, Amanda, who gave me her time, was my cheerleader, and made my work better. And finally, thank you to my editor, Nicole Frail. You believed in this book and me. You gave me this opportunity that I never knew I was a possibility and helped me bring this book into the world. Thank you everybody at Skyhorse, for all of your work behind the scenes.

ABOUT THE AUTHOR

© Rhiannon Connelly

Rachel is a registered psychologist and parenting expert who lives in Perth, Australia, with her husband, daughter, and two goofy boxer dogs. She has lived in England and Australia, working extensively with children and families in general counseling, domestic violence and trauma counseling, play therapy and in environments such as women's refuge, educational settings, and children's residential homes. Rachel has delivered presentations at national conferences and university guest lectures on topics such as play therapy, domestic violence, and trauma. Rachel also works closely with journalists in Australia, United States, and the United Kingdom, providing expert commentary on a variety of mental health topics, relationships, child development, and parenting.

INDEX